D1809679

Product Gems 1

101 Science Experiments That
Demonstrate How to Build Products
People Love

David Greenwood

How AT&T got customers to love them again, why Dollar
Shave Club subscribers keep coming back for more, how
Patagonia's use of organic cotton led to sales
skyrocketing, and over 100 more examples of the
psychology behind the most successful products ever
created.

Product Gems distils research from 73 behavioural science
papers and case-studies into 111 bite-size "gems" that
demonstrate the key techniques used by leading
companies to build products people love.

Copyright © 2018 by David Greenwood

All rights reserved. No part of this book may be reproduced, scanned, or distributed in any printed or electronic form without permission. Please do not participate in or encourage piracy of copyrighted materials in violation of the author's rights. Purchase only authorised editions.

For Dad. The most irrational person I know!

Contents

0.1. The Science Behind the Book

How each chapter has been carefully designed

Academic research papers offer fascinating insights into the way we think and behave. While they are full of incredible pieces of information, finding the relevant papers, understanding the terminology, and then figuring out how the findings can be put into action is very time-consuming.

The time investment required to digest research results in many companies overlooking the latest research entirely, with innovation suffering as a result. This book aims to solve this problem by distilling academic papers down into easy-to-read chapters to help decision makers quickly understand how the latest discoveries can help them develop, position, sell, and support their products.

I've divided the chapters down into clear sections (easy, intermediate, advanced, actionable) to help readers easily pick out content relevant to them. Each chapter gradually elaborates on the subject, or gem, to include more focused research. The chapters conclude with a series of Products Gems, actionable information from the research discussed.

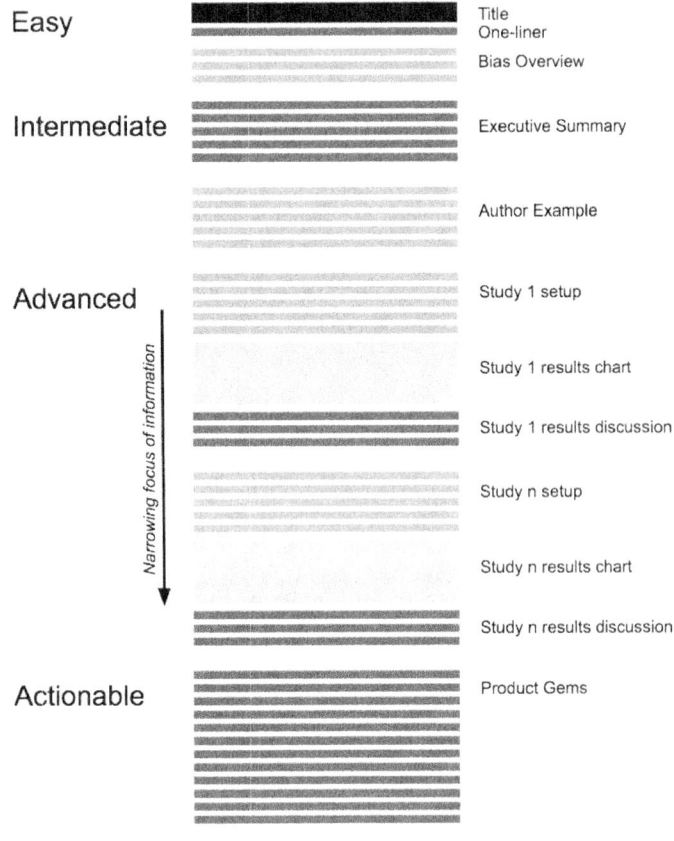

Easy — Title / One-liner / Bias Overview

Intermediate — Executive Summary

Author Example

Advanced — Study 1 setup

Narrowing focus of information

Study 1 results chart

Study 1 results discussion

Study n setup

Study n results chart

Study n results discussion

Actionable — Product Gems

Easy

Easy

Title
One-liner

Bias Overview

You might be familiar with the acronym, tl;dr (too long, didn't read). Some readers will want to skim through information to help them hone in on what they're looking for or to perhaps quickly refresh their memory on a subject. The first few sentences of each chapter include the title (the subject), a one-line description of it, and an overview paragraph written to provide a brief introduction that can be grasped quickly.

Intermediate

Intermediate

Executive Summary

Author Example

Before jumping straight into the research, an executive summary is used to prime readers on the topic. Essentially, this is an elaboration on the overview. A "real-world" example of the subject is also demonstrated before more complex academic discussion is introduced.

Advanced

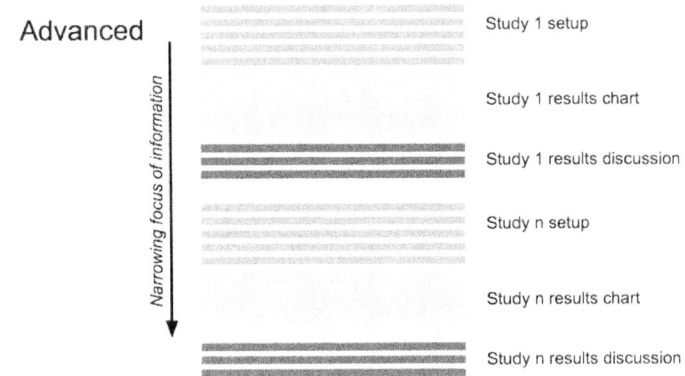

The advanced section examines specific academic studies, describing the setup, the results, and what they mean. Graphs and charts are used to display the results from each study because research suggests that "illustrated text" is more easily understood that "non-illustrated text". It also allows the reader to quickly share the insights learned from an experiment more easily with others outside of this book.

Depending on the subject, a varying number of studies are introduced. The idea being that as the chapter progresses, the research will become more focused on specific areas of the subject and the nuances and limitations associated with it.

Actionable

The ultimate goal of each chapter is to provide readers with information they can take away and use. Each Product Gem is designed so it can be read before the content of the chapter and still be easily understood—and more importantly, be put into practice. If you read one part of each chapter, make sure it's the Product Gems.

0.2. Introduction

We're All Predictably Irrational

Every day we make around 35,000 conscious decisions, perhaps many more according to some researchers. You assume you're intelligent and capable. You assume you're logical. You assume that the decisions you make are the result of experience and careful consideration.

The fact is, the human brain is deeply flawed. There are some things you aren't very good at and never will be. Evidence of our weaknesses exists everywhere. Calculators, notepads, to-do lists, calendars, alarm clocks. There are hundreds of inventions and applications on the market that are specifically designed to make up for the brain's shortcomings. We're regularly reminded that we're not computers.

As emotional creatures, feelings tend to cloud our judgements and lead to irrational choices. In the heat of debate, words can be exchanged, that, no sooner than leaving one's mouth are instantly regretted.

Our brains are the result of tens of thousands of years of evolution. In many circumstances, they prove to be well-oiled machines. Every day, we rely on our brain's mental shortcuts, or heuristics, when making decisions. Heuristics are quick, informal, and intuitive algorithms our brains use to generate an approximate answer to a reasoning question.

For the most part, heuristics are helpful because they allow us to make sense of a complex environment quickly, but there are times when they fail at making a correct assessment of the world.

Cognitive biases are the tendency to think in certain ways, often resulting in a deviation from rational, logical decision-making that heuristics typically produce. They are little quirks that make us all human. We are often unaware of our own cognitive biases and how significantly they affect our lives. These biases affect the way we go about our lives; from the brand of toothpaste we use, the route we take to work, or even the people we associate with.

During the last century, psychologists have examined many of our cognitive weaknesses to get a better understanding of how and why we behave in the ways we do. Entire fields of expertise exist to make up for a gulf in our abilities. Companies now employ teams responsible for helping them better understand their consumers. In many cases, our decisions follow clear patterns that have long been understood.

Diamonds, the world's most popular gem by sales volume, are the result of a carefully thought-out campaign that tugs at many of our cognitive biases. By creating the illusion of scarcity, despite the gem being one of the most abundant on earth, diamond companies created a whole new market. The scarcity heuristic leads us to value rare objects higher than those in greater supply and is the reason why many of us are willing to pay significant sums of money for diamond engagement rings despite the fact they will lose 50% of their value once they leave the jewellery store.

Cognitive biases also affect the decisions you and your team make in a professional capacity, too. They affect your ability to perform rational research, your ability to analyse test results, the way you market your product, or how successful your meetings are. Disagree? That's your blind spot bias at play, a bias that causes you to view yourself as less biased than other people.

We're all in this together. These are our shared mental stumbling blocks. Use what you learn as you navigate this book to understand how, as humans, we're predictably irrational. For readers looking to be enlightened about human behaviour, you will be rewarded with *Product Gems* that will help improve not only the success of your products but also your own success.

While this book won't eradicate your biases, or indeed those of your customers, it will provide some concrete, counterintuitive, and fascinating insights that you can use to account for them.

Let me start by getting my foot in the door...

1. Foot-in-the-Door Technique

Once someone has agreed to a small request, they are more likely to agree to a larger request

The foot-in-the-door technique involves getting a someone to agree to a large request by creating a sense of obligation by setting them up to agree to a smaller, more modest request first.

In the days of door-to-door sales (remember those?), getting your foot in the door meant exactly that. If a salesperson got their foot inside the door, the unwitting prospect couldn't slam it in their face, and the chance of a sale was drastically improved.

In the modern world, getting your foot in the door might appear difficult. Readers working in telesales will be all too familiar with being hung up on before they've managed finished their first sentence. Online sellers might never even know a prospect has visited their website.

Even though the days of door-to-door salespeople are coming to an end, some of their persuasion and sales techniques remain effective, including the foot-in-the-door technique.

Can I take just five minutes of your time?

Teenagers

Most teenagers are subconscious masters of the foot-in-the-door technique. Let me recall a common discussion I would have with my father as a teenager that highlights the use of the technique:

> *[Teenage Me] Dad, can I go out for an hour to see Sam?*
> *[Dad] Yes.*
> *[Me] I just called Sam and he's going to the cinema—can I go with him?*
> *[Dad] Hmmm, OK.*
> *[Me] I haven't got money—could you lend me enough to get in?*
> *[Dad] Sure, but just this once.*
> *[Me] Can you pick us up afterwards?*
> *[Dad] I suppose so.*

Now, imagine if I had combined such an ask into a single request; asking to go out, borrow money, and be picked up. Do you think I would have been successful? Maybe, but research would suggest that I would have more luck by breaking down the request into smaller, individual parts, with the largest request being made last. In doing so, I made it harder for my Dad to say, "No!" due to an existing sense of obligation.

The foot-in-the-door technique uses commitment and consistency to elicit compliance.

Household Items

In 1966, two researchers set up an experiment where they contacted 156 women by telephone asking them to each conduct a series of tasks to test this theory (Freedman & Fraser, 1966).

The participants were split into two groups. Initially, one group of participants was contacted with a small request; to answer eight questions about household products they used (small request). Three days later, both groups were contacted by the same researcher and asked to undertake a larger request; to allow six men to come and take an inventory of all the products in their home (large request).

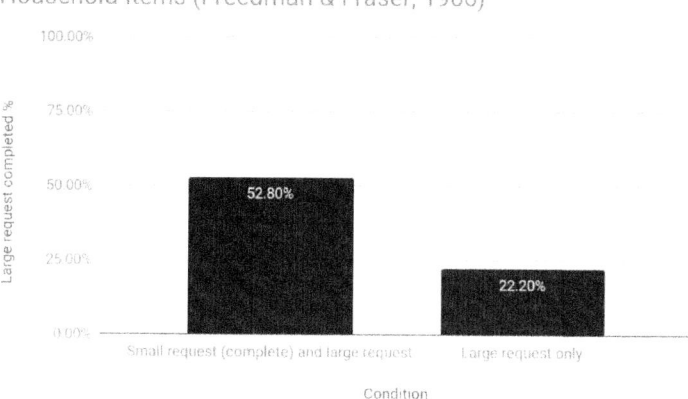

Household Items (Freedman & Fraser, 1966)

Astoundingly, 52.8% of the participants who first completed the small request subsequently agreed to allow the group of men to rummage through their house and catalogue the products they owned! In contrast, only 22.2% of the participants who were contacted just once (to complete the large request) agreed to the same large request.

The results of the experiment clearly show the technique in action: people are more likely to agree or comply with larger requests if they've agreed to a modest one first.

Support the Cause

The two researchers realised that their first experiment might suggest requests were more likely to succeed when the person making both requests was familiar to the participant and if the second request was similar to the first (as opposed to asking for something completely different).

To validate these theories, both researchers conducted a second experiment, this time visiting 112 homeowners in-person (Freedman & Fraser, 1966).

About half of the homeowners were first approached by a researcher claiming to be from the "Community Committee for Traffic Safety" or the "Keep California Beautiful Committee". Each homeowner was asked by the researcher to display a small sign in their front window, either "Be a Safe Driver" or "Keep California Beautiful", depending on the committee the researcher claimed to represent (small request).

Two weeks later, a new researcher approached all the homeowners posing to be a member of the "Citizens for Safe Driving" organisation (a different organisation to the "Community Committee for Traffic Safety"). On this occasion, each homeowner was asked to place large, unattractive "Drive Carefully" sign in their front garden for a week (large request).

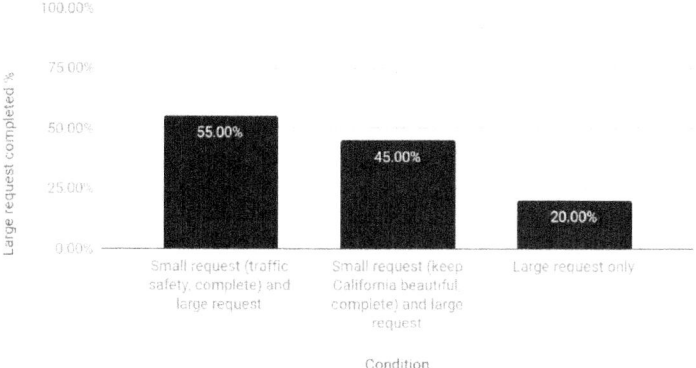

Support the Cause (Freedman & Fraser, 1966)

When just the large request was made, only 20% agreed to put the oversized, ugly sign in their front garden. In contrast, 55% of homeowners who first agreed to display a small sign from the "Community Committee for Traffic Safety" subsequently agreed to display the ugly sign for a similar organisation, "Citizens for Safe Driving".

What's more, even when the second request was made by a completely different organisation, cause, and person to the first—as was the case for the group of homeowners first approached by the "Keep California Beautiful Committee"—45% of those who completed the small request then agreed to the second larger request from a different committee, the "Citizens for Safe Driving".

The foot-in-the-door technique can be effective even when the two requests are for completely different issues, or from two different people.

Rewarding Recycling

The previous experiment studied innocuous requests from a non-profit group with socially conscious goals. Researchers hypothesised that because these requests were prosocial, a phenomenon where people help each other with no thought of reward or compensation (although perhaps an improved sense of self-image), the likelihood of success of the foot-in-the-door technique was increased as a result. However, the foot-in-the-door technique can be used to equal effect in the commercial world, as the next experiment demonstrates.

In the experiment, researchers first split 315 participants into five groups (Scott, 1977). The first four groups all received a small request asking them to put a small sign promoting recycling in their front window. Each group was offered a different cash incentive for doing so, either $0, $1, or $3.

Two weeks later, all five groups were contacted and asked to comply with a moderate second request (to address 25 letters) or large second request (to address 75 letters) related to the recycling campaign. This time, only one group ("double incentive") was offered an incentive for completing the large second request.

Rewarding Recycling (Scott, 1977)

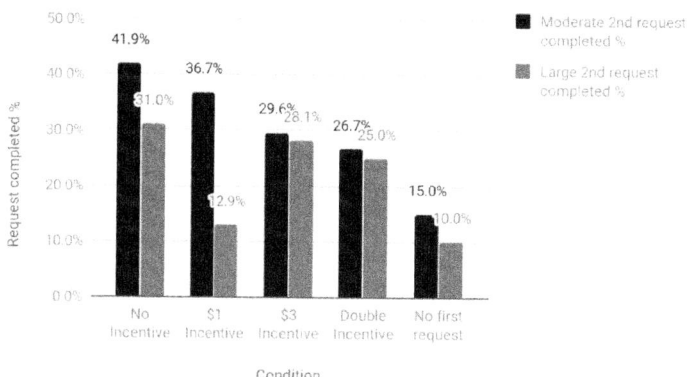

Completion of the second request was lowest in the group where no small first request was made; 15.0% for the moderate request and 10.0% for the large request.

The participants in the group that completed a small request when no incentive was offered were 41.9% and 31.0% likely to complete the moderate and large second requests respectively. Generally, the greater the incentive offered, the lower the compliance. Only 26.7% and 25.0% of participants offered a monetary incentive for both tasks completed the first and second request for the moderate and large tasks respectively.

The foot-in-the-door technique was most effective without the use of monetary incentive strategies in producing compliance.

Email for Help

Recent studies have tested these findings with similar (albeit less dramatic) results. In one such experiment, researchers posed as statistics students from a university (Guéguen et al., 2002).

The researchers sent emails to fifty-eight real students studying at one university. Participants were split into two groups. Researchers sent one group of students an email asking for help:

"I have to send my CV to a company in a Word RTF format. I don't know how it works, can you help me?"

A second email was then sent to all the groups. The second email asked for help but this time to complete a questionnaire, a task that would take significantly longer to complete than the first request sent to half of the participants.

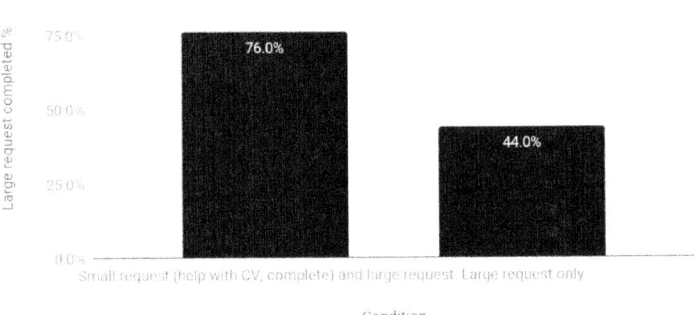

Email for Help (Guéguen et al., 2002)

In both conditions, compliance was relatively high. Of the participants who completed the first request for help with a CV, 76% of them then completed the longer questionnaire sent afterwards. Only 44% of those who received a request to complete the long questionnaire, but not help with a CV, actually completed it.

People are more likely to agree or comply with larger requests if they've agreed to a modest one first. The delivery method is not a major factor in producing compliance when using the foot-in-the-door technique -- electronic messages can be used just as effectively.

Product Gems

1. **Know your customer**
   Specifically; what are their aspirations? If you can align your requests to their self-image, perhaps becoming an expert in the area of business your product fits, you are likely to have greater success with the foot-in-the-door technique.

2. **Be creative**
   The foot-in-the-door technique is nothing new. Make sure your small request is not overlooked amongst the competition. I was recently asked to sign up for a company's newsletter (small request). The options presented were "Sign up, I want to get smarter" or "Don't sign up, I don't want to get smarter". Keep in mind; the foot-in-the-door technique works best when both requests are consistent.

3. **Encourage public commitments**
   If a someone agrees to complete a small request, make sure they complete it, or the foot-in-the-door technique won't work. Getting them to do this publically adds a sense of commitment to a group, meaning they'll be less likely to back out (social proof). This technique works very effectively in assigning follow-up items during meetings.

4. **Stay committed**
   Longer product sales cycles generally tend to involve more touch points with your prospects. Try to build small requests into every contact you have with them. Over time, their sense of commitment to you will increase with each request, ultimately making it harder for them to say no when you come to close the deal.

5. **Don't stop requesting**
   A closed deal could be used as a completed small request. Researchers have found agreeing to purchase something at a given price increases the likelihood of agreeing to purchase it at a higher price (Cialdini et al., 1975). Think about how you could upsell after the first deal. Or potentially shrink the initial deal size to improve the odds of closing a much larger deal later.

6. **Make requests engaging**
   While a small action can induce the feeling of wanting to remain consistent, experiments have shown that people who go through a great deal of trouble or pain to attain something tend to value it more highly than those who attain the same thing with a minimum of effort (effort justification). Don't make your small requests too easy.

7. **Reward prospects, but not with promotions**
   Instead of using costly discounts or promotions, think about how you could incorporate the foot-in-the-door technique into your marketing. If you're pitching at a trade show, ask for a business card in return for a demonstration of your product.

8. **Leverage the competition**
   The cunning advertisers amongst you will want to promote your product to a consumer even after they have purchased a similar product from a competitor, knowing that by doing so can inhibit closure and increase the chances of them switching to your brand for future purchases.

9. **Charities pay close attention**
   Again, think about your prospect's self-image. Most people want to be (or at least appear to be) compassionate, which you can use to your

advantage. Use small prosocial requests like signing a petition before larger requests that might include asking for monetary donations (see: prosocial effect).

2. Category Size Bias

We're more influenced by options presented in a relatively large group

Consumers perceptions of risk and probability are influenced not only by the number of categories into which possible outcomes are classified but also by category size.

I recently watched a competitive swimming heat on television. The race sticks in my mind because 50% of the athletes, four in total, were from the United States. Knowing very little about each participant, nor who the favourite was for the race, at first glance, it looked like the United States had to place in the top three. The result: none of them finished in the top three.

In this case, the size of each category, the country each athlete represented, incorrectly led me to believe they had a better chance of making it into the top three. I incorrectly believed "they had the numbers on their side".

The category size bias demonstrates how our probability judgments are often inaccurate. Category size can impact the perceived likelihood of a specific outcome, such that an outcome classified into a large (vs small) category is perceived as more likely to occur.

Creating and sizing categories has a huge potential to influence and motivate long-lasting behavioural change.

Roulette Wheel

I don't visit casinos very often, but when I do, Roulette is one of the few games I like to gamble on. For those unfamiliar, a Roulette wheel has eighteen black slots, eighteen red slots and two green slots.

The probability of landing on any of the slots is exactly the same. However, many of us make the mistake of thinking that the ball is more likely to land on a specific black or red number than on a specific green number. This is because there are more black and red slots (eighteen each) than green slots (two). Imagine a Roulette wheel with no colours and try to guess where the ball is most likely to land. It's impossible. The probability of landing on any slot is identical.

When standing in front of the Roulette table, our rational judgment of the probability of landing on a 'red 7', for instance, is affected by the category it sits within. Red is a bigger category than green, so we assume it to be the more probable of the two.

We mistakenly believe items in larger categories to be more likely to occur than ones in smaller categories.

Lottery Balls

In an experiment examining how we judged probabilities, 223 participants were split into two groups and asked to evaluate one of two versions of a lottery (Isaac & Brough, 2014). In both versions, participants were asked to judge the probability of randomly selecting a specific coloured ball from a bag containing fifteen balls, each of which were labelled with a different number from 1 to 15.

The version of the lottery shown to the first group used five black, five grey and five white balls (small category). The second group were shown a version that used two black, eleven grey and two white balls (large category).

In each version, the participants were asked the percentage likelihood of choosing the "grey 8" ball from the bag.

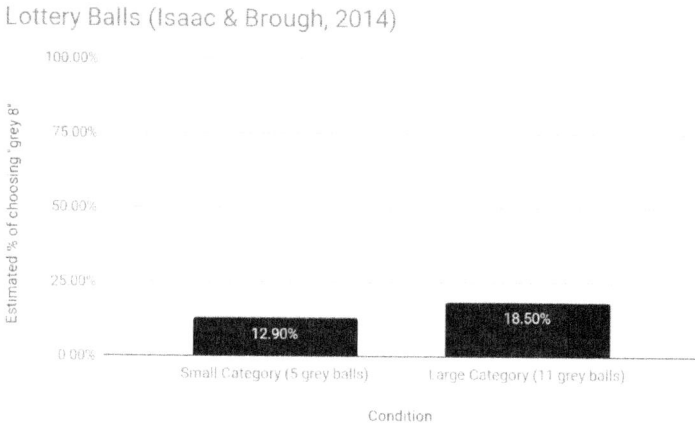

Lottery Balls (Isaac & Brough, 2014)

In both games, the actual probability of selecting the "grey 8" ball was the same, 1/15 (6.7%), although in the second version, the grey balls were in a relatively large category when compared to the first version.

Participants believed they were more likely to choose the "grey 8" when eleven of the fifteen balls in the bag were grey (18.5%) compared to when only five of the balls were grey (12.9%). Similar to the Roulette example, because there were more grey balls than black or white in the second version, participants thought that the "grey 8" ball was more likely to come up.

This first experiment shows that when outcomes are put into relatively large categories, we often (incorrectly) believe they're more likely to occur.

Lottery Tickets

Another similar study aimed to show that the category size bias occurs even when category size is approximated rather than explicitly provided and that it can affect not only probability estimates but also the amount we're willing to risk to obtain the outcome.

In this experiment, eighty-one participants were shown a glass bowl that contained exactly ninety folded lottery tickets, eighty-one of which were blue and nine of which were yellow, although no numbers were disclosed to the participants (Isaac & Brough, 2014).

Students were randomly assigned one of these blue (large category) or yellow tickets (small category) to put into the hat as the last entry (ninety-one tickets total) and asked both how likely it was that their ticket would be chosen. They also were asked how much they'd like to bet (between $0 and $10) and told the winner would receive a cash reward of one-hundred times his or her wager amount.

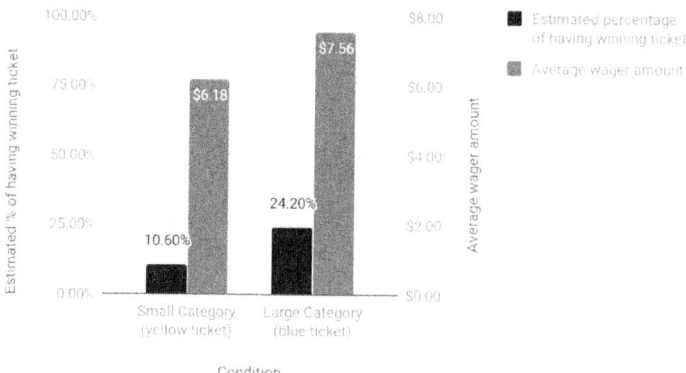

Lottery Tickets (Isaac & Brough, 2014)

The mathematical probability of selecting any individual ticket was 1/91 (1.1%) regardless of variations in colour. However, those with blue tickets—of which there were eighty-two in the pot when the draw was made—believed they had a 24.2% of choosing their one blue ticket! Compare that to yellow ticket holders—of which there were ten in the pot when the draw was made—who believed their chance of choosing their ticket and thus winning was only 10.6%.

As in the lottery balls experiment, these results show that we feel more confident in choosing something if it's put within a relatively large category.

Interestingly, participants were also willing to wager 24%, or $1.38 more, if their ticket was part of the large category compared to the small category ($6.18 vs $7.56)! We're more likely to take higher risks if the outcome is put within a relatively large category.

Dice Roll

Researchers also wanted to test the magnitude of the bias. Put another way, to test if a large category size increased the estimated probability of an outcome occurring. To test this, 175 participants were asked to judge the probability of rolling the letter "A" or "T" on a fair twenty-six-sided die that displayed each letter of the English alphabet on one of its sides (Isaac & Brough, 2014).

The researchers first split the participants into three groups, each receiving a different amount of information about the task:

1. The first group were explicitly informed that there were five vowels and twenty-one consonants on the die and were asked to estimate the probability of rolling either "vowel A" or "consonant T" (high communication).
2. The participants in the second group were asked to estimate the probability of rolling either "vowel A" or "consonant T," but this time the sizes of each category were not explicitly stated (medium communication).
3. Finally, the third group was asked to estimate the probability of rolling either "letter A" or the "letter T" (low communication).

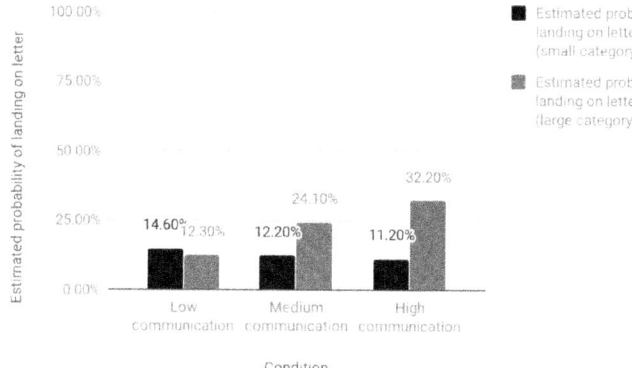

Dice Roll (Isaac & Brough, 2014)

The actual probability of rolling any individual letter was 1/26 (3.8%). The researchers found that when actively mentioning group size—T was one of 21 consonants in the alphabet and A was one of five vowels—participants believed that the letter "T" was more likely to be rolled (M = 32.2%) than the letter "A" (M = 11.2%). In contrast, the low information group where category size was not disclosed believed the probability of rolling a letter "T" or letter "A" to be much more even (M = 14.6% and M = 12.3% respectively), although still significantly higher than the actual probability.

The more clearly the difference in category size is highlighted, the more likely we are to choose something from the larger category.

IT Security

In one final experiment, the researchers wanted to explore the ability of the category size bias to influence behaviour change. In this experiment, 171 participants completed an online study about IT security threats (Isaac & Brough,

2014). Each participant was given a list of nine IT security behaviours. Behaviours included "change password" and "backup data".

They were then asked to place these nine tasks into one of two categories: "identity theft" or "loss of data". Participants were told one category would need to end up with seven items (large category), and the other with two items (small category).

Researchers then followed up with all participants to examine how many of the behaviours participants had implemented during the three months following the first part of the experiment.

IT Security (Isaac & Brough, 2014)

Preventative behaviour	Mean likelihood of performing each behaviour during the next three months (1 = very unlikely, 7 = very likely)	
	Large category	Small Category
Change password	5.24	4.28
Encrypt sensitive file	3.76	3.58
Use pop-up blocker or firewall	6.36	6.32
Use password-protected screensaver	4.89	3.22
Install (or maintain) security software with automatic updates	6.07	5.37
Verify the publisher before downloading and installing software	5.94	5.52
Use antivirus or anti-spy software	6.46	5
Avoid opening unsolicited email attachments	6.65	6.32
Back up data	5.53	4.91
All	*5.74*	*4.49*

In the three months following the exercise, participants were overall more likely to engage in those preventative behaviours that they'd classified into a large category of tasks (M = 5.74) than the small category of tasks (M = 4.49). For some behaviours, for example, to use antivirus or anti-spy software, participants were over 20% more likely to adopt it when they placed it into the larger category.

It would appear the participants believed the IT security threats associated with a large number of preventive behaviours were more likely to happen than ones associated with a smaller number of preventative behaviours.

We are more likely to take action when tasks are in a comparatively larger list.

Product Gems

1. **Communicating category size to influence**
   Highlighting the differences between the large and small categories is highly likely to enhance the effect of the category size bias. A software product stating that there are ten features in the premium version versus four in the free version will help nudge a decision towards the premium version (be careful of the choice paradox though).

2. **Use different techniques to categorise and influence**
   You can use a number of elements to suggest that items belong to one category or another: colour, size, shape, typography, etc. The greater emphasis people perceive between large and smaller groups can sway their decisions.

3. **Foster confident risk taking and decision making**
   As the blue and yellow lottery ticket example shows, we're likely to take more risks and have a greater level of confidence in choosing something from a larger group, than from a relatively smaller one. Use the category size bias to increase your customer's appetite to spend more (perceived risk). Gambling companies take note.

4. **Create a sense of belonging**
   The category size bias provides a credible explanation for why we tend to associate with large groups that are viewed favourably by society. Being part of a large and "desirable" social group can make others believe that we also possess the qualities of its members. For small businesses, it suggests that forming or being a part of a

consortium or large and high-quality networking group can dramatically elevate your brand image.

5. **Shape long-term behaviour changes**
   Research suggests that when crafting health-related messages, grouping a preventable disease such as lung cancer with a larger number of other potential health risks would positively impact decision making. This is based on the idea that a reader will believe they are more likely to contract a disease from a larger group of health risks, with lung cancer being one of them.

3. Choice Paradox

Limiting options significantly increases successful purchasing decisions and reduces customer regret

Whilst some choice is good, it doesn't mean more choice is necessarily better. In fact, an overabundance of choice can actually negatively impact our very well being.

"Monstromart: where shopping is a baffling ordeal" reads the slogan of a fictional supermarket in The Simpsons.

Inside the supermarket, there were whole aisles for one type of product. There were different brands of tomato ketchup as far as the eye could see, bags sugar could be bought in hundreds of varieties, the express checkout had a sign reading: "1,000 items or less".

In the end, the Simpsons returned to Apu's Kwik-E-Mart. In doing so, the Simpsons were making a choice to reduce their choice. It wasn't quite a rational choice, but it made sense. Their unconstrained freedom left them paralysed to make decisions.

There is no denying choice improves the quality of our lives. When people have no choice, life is almost unbearable. Choice is essentially freedom, which is fundamental to our well-being. However, like The Simpsons, the choice paradox suggests that offering consumers too much choice can leave them paralysed to make a decision.

Clothes Shopping

In one of the most comprehensive books on the subject, aptly titled, The Paradox of Choice (Schwartz, 2009), Schwartz describes his frustration when shopping for a new pair of jeans. His expectation was simply to buy a regular pair of jeans, similar to the pair he already owned, although in better condition. Schwartz recalls being asked by the sales assistant:

> *"Do you want them slim fit, easy fit, relaxed fit, baggy, or extra baggy? Do you want them stonewashed, acid-washed, or distressed? Do you want them button-fly or zipper-fly? Do you want them faded or regular?"*

After eventually narrowing his choices down by trying them all on, he managed to choose a pair he thought was right for him. Leaving the store, he questioned if he'd made the right decision. Then his rational brain kicked in, and Schwartz realised how little importance was riding on his decision but wondered why buying a pair of jeans had become a daylong project.

By creating these different options for consumers, the shop has undoubtedly helped customers with varied tastes and body types where just one style of jeans may have existed before. Though this choice has introduced a new problem. Schwartz summarises:

> *"As the number of choices keeps growing, negative aspects of having a multitude of options begin to appear. As the number of choices grows further, the negatives escalate until we become*

overloaded. At this point, choice no longer liberates, but debilitates."

Jam Jars

In arguably one of the most cited experiments studying the choice paradox, researchers set up a display featuring a line of exotic, high-quality jams in a gourmet retail supermarket known for its product variety (Iyengar & Lepper, 2001). Customers could taste the jams and were given a dollar off if they bought a jar.

One group was able to taste six jams. In another group, twenty-four varieties were available to taste. In either case, all twenty-four varieties were available for purchase afterwards.

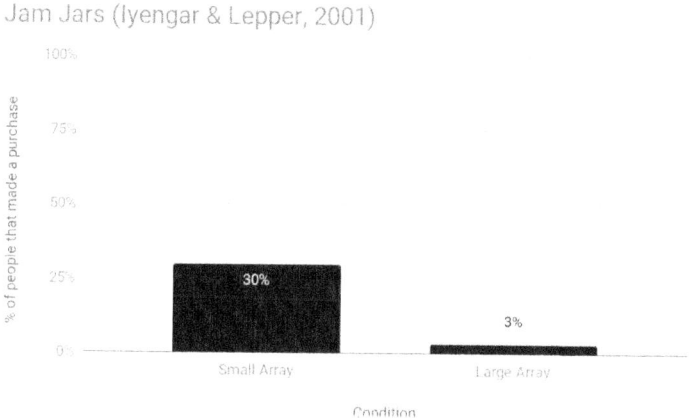

The large array of jams attracted more people to the table than the small array, though in both cases people tasted the same number of jams on average. When it came to buying, a staggering 30% of people exposed to the small array of jams actually bought a jar. Only 3% of those exposed to the large array of jams did so!

The study clearly demonstrates a consumer choice paralysis. When a large number of similar choices are available, the decision to choose becomes harder.

Movie Essays

The researchers also wanted to explore how an overabundance of choice can demotivate us. To study this, they set up an experiment where 197 participants were asked to write an essay about a movie they had watched (Iyengar & Lepper, 2001).

After watching the movie, participants were split into two groups. One group was given six essay topics to choose from (small array), while the other group was given thirty potential essay topics (large array) they could choose to write about.

Researchers then studied and graded the number of essays completed by each group.

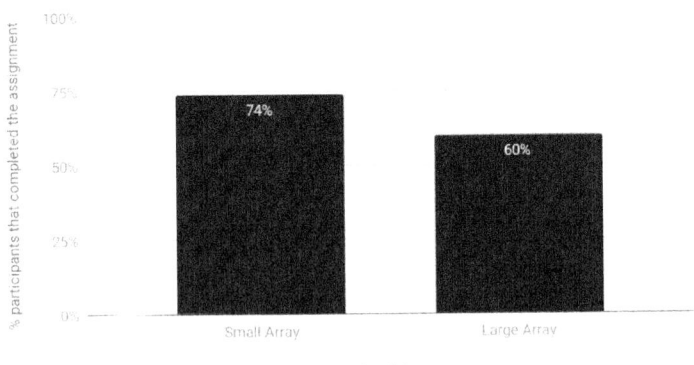

Movie Essays (Iyengar & Lepper, 2001)

Overall, 65% of the students chose to do the assignment. Of the students provided with only six topics, 74% turned in the assignment. In contrast, only 60% of the students provided with thirty topics to choose from completed the assignment.

The students seemed to be more motivated when their choices were limited, and what's more, they even performed better in such circumstances producing higher graded essays overall.

Gourmet Chocolates

Another study by the same researchers examined potential dissatisfaction in decision making when an extensive choice was offered. This time, 134 college students were asked to evaluate a variety of gourmet chocolates (Iyengar & Lepper, 2001).

The students were first asked to choose which chocolate—based on description and appearance—they would choose for themselves. One group of students was shown a choice of six chocolates. The other group was shown thirty chocolates to choose from. All students then tasted and rated the chocolate they selected.

After making all their selections, participants were asked to rate how satisfied they were with the chocolate they had selected on a scale that ranged from 1 (not at all) to 7 (extremely). Finally, in a different room, the students were offered a small box of chocolates in lieu of cash as payment for their participation.

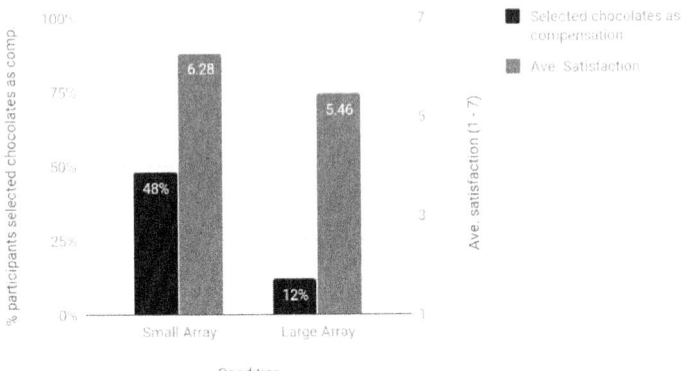

Gourmet Chocolates (Iyengar & Lepper, 2001)

It turns out that the participants faced with the small array of chocolates were more satisfied (M = 6.28) with their tasting than those faced with the large array (M = 5.46). Not only that, but they were also four times as likely to choose chocolates over cash compensation for their participation.

The results might seem counterintuitive at first glance. You might think you'll find something you like better from a set of twenty-four or thirty options than from a set of six. Though it appears there is a balance. Reduced choice can actually improve our satisfaction.

The Ultimatum Game

Economists and psychologists have been investigating the relationship between regret and choice since the early 1980s. In one such experiment, forty-six students volunteered to take part in an ultimatum game (Zeelenberg & Beattie, 1997).

An ultimatum game involves a person proposing how to divide a sum of money between themselves and another person. The other person then chooses to either accept or reject this proposal. If the offer is rejected, neither player walks away with any money.

For this experiment, each student was told to divide one hundred Dutch Guilders between themselves and another player (simulated by a computer) who would accept or reject the offer.

The students were split into two groups. Depending on which group they were placed in, the participants then learned that their offer was accepted and they could have offered two Guilders less, or that their offer was accepted and they could have offered ten Guilders less.

They were then asked to rate on a 7-point scale from 0 (no regret) to 7 (total regret) how much regret they experienced when comparing their own offer to the minimum acceptable offer.

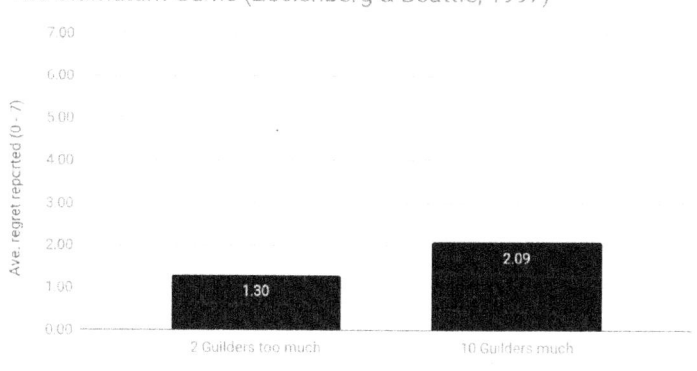

The Ultimatum Game (Zeelenberg & Beattie, 1997)

The group who were told their offers were only slightly higher than the minimum acceptable offer (two Guilders more) suffered lower levels of regret (M = 1.30) than the group who were told their offer was much higher than the minimum acceptable offer (10 Guilders more) (M = 2.09).

The study suggests we consider the possibility of future regret and take it into account when making decisions. In the experiment, the students were motivated to avoid or minimise post-decision regret. By introducing more choice, our ability to avoid regret becomes harder.

Art Posters

Researchers have also studied how people make decisions and concluded there are two basic styles:

1. "Maximisers" like to take their time and weigh a wide range of options—sometimes every possible one—before choosing. Maximisers will often feel pressure to choose the "best" possible option from an overwhelming array of choices rather than simply settle for "good enough".
2. "Satisficers" would rather be fast than thorough; they prefer to quickly choose the option that meets the minimum criteria.

Given this, you would expect maximisers to suffer from the choice paradox more severely than satisficers. Numerous experiments have been carried out exploring the behaviour of maximisers and satisficers.

In another experiment by a different researcher, sixty students were first asked to complete a questionnaire designed to assess their decision-making style (Shiner, 2015). Questions included: "When I watch TV, I channel surf, often scanning through the available options even while attempting to watch one program" and "I never settle for second best". Based on these answers, the researchers categorised each student as a maximiser or a satisficer.

An experimenter then presented the students with nine posters showing paintings by famous artists. The students were asked to rank the posters in order of their personal preference. Next, the experimenter told the participants that there were extra copies of the third and fourth-ranked posters and asked them which of the two they'd like to take home.

The satisficer and maximiser groups were then both split in half. In half of each group, participants were told they could change their minds about their selection and switch posters at any time during the following month (reversible decision). In the other half of each group, the experimenter told the students that their choice of a poster was final and they would not be able to change it (irreversible decision).

After making all their selections, participants were asked to rate how satisfied they were with the poster they had selected on a scale that ranged from 1 (not at all) to 7 (extremely).

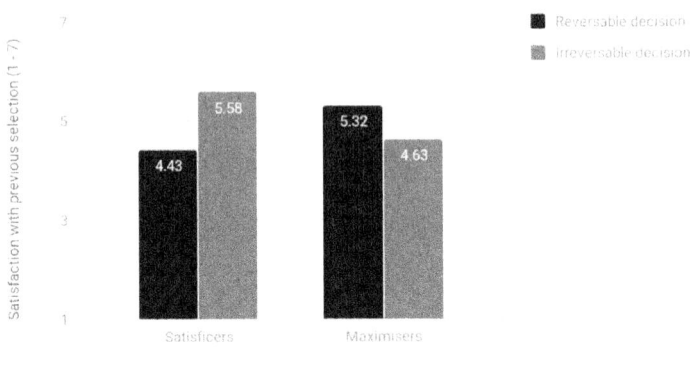

Art Posters (Shiner, 2015)

As expected, the satisficers reported more satisfaction with their poster choices when the decision was irreversible (M = 5.58) rather than reversible (M = 4.43), while maximisers were happier when the decision was reversible (M = 5.32) rather than irreversible (M = 4.63).

It would seem that maximisers greater tendency to experience regret extends to situations involving anticipated regret as well, as their behaviour appeared to be aimed at minimising the possibility of later regret. Anticipated regret could be even worse, because it can produce not just dissatisfaction but a choice paralysis.

Product Gems

1. **Experiment with choices**
   Think hard about the minimum amount of choice you need in order to clearly differentiate your brand from the competition. Look back ten years and compare Apple's newly released iPhone product range with Nokia's. Choice can be a confusing burden as much as a convenience.

2. **Trust in the choices offered**
   Too much choice can be perceived as a lack of confidence in your own brand. Being asked twelve different questions about how you want your burrito will be cognitively tiring and leave many wondering why the company can't be more bold and self-assured with respect to its product.

3. **Guide the buyer to a decision**
   Streamline choice architecture to encourage some sort of 'good' decision where one would otherwise not take place at all. For instance, reducing choice and consumer apathy within a user flow at key intervals where drop-off has been found to be high will increase conversions. In the case of online retailers seeing customers leaving at the checkout, a reduction in payment methods might be beneficial.

4. **Increased consumer choice = increased product costs**
   You'll have to work harder and spend more to market the differences between the products in your range, the more choice you offer.

5. **Monitor customer satisfaction**
   Heightened regret and diminished happiness may result when too many product options are offered.

Think carefully about target consumers for each product option and ensure they don't overlap.

6. **Think like a maximiser**

   Every decision you fail to take to focus and simplify your range is one more that your customers will be burdened with, every single time. In the case of maximisers, this can lead to anticipated regret (i.e., paralysed to make a buying decision) and actual regret (i.e., leading to brand damage or low renewal rates).

4. Choice-Supportive Bias

We tend to remember our choices as better than they actually were

When we recall a past decision, we distort memories to make the choices we made appear to be the best that could be made. Thus, when we have selected from a set of options, we will attribute more positive and less negative attributes to the option we have chosen.

Every four years citizens in the United States cast their vote for the next president. The U.S. presidential election of 2000 saw George Bush of the Republican party face-off against Al Gore representing the Democrats in a bid for the White House.

On the election night of 2000, it was unclear who had won, with the electoral votes of the state of Florida still undecided. The returned votes showed that Bush had won Florida by such a close margin that state law required a recount. A month-long series of legal battles led to the contentious, 5–4 Supreme Court decision of Bush v. Gore, which ended the recount. With the end of the recount, Bush won Florida by a margin of .009% or 537 votes.

Bush's 8-year term saw the horrific events of September 11th and the controversial wars in Afghanistan and Iraq that followed. Many Bush supporters still focus on the positives of his presidency as a justification for his actions, whilst opposing Democrats will argue their candidate, Gore, would have handled the situation better.

We can often ignore opposing evidence in favour of what we believe is correct (see: confirmation bias). Once we've made a decision based on the evidence considered, we don't like looking like we made the wrong one. To help ensure this, we often over-attribute positive features to the options we've chosen and negative features to options not chosen, like political candidates. As a result, we feel good about ourselves and our choices, and have less regret for bad decisions. This makes changing people's incorrect beliefs an incredibly hard task.

Consumers desire for past choices to be rational and well-made (or at least seem to be) makes them more likely to overlook any faults in an effort to convince themselves and others that they made the right decision.

Dollar Shave Club

29-years young at the time of writing, I have a confession to make; I still struggle to grow a beard. Even during my school years, many of my friends sprouted bushy and lustrous beards. I don't think I bought a razor until my university years. While I'm not a particularly credible voice on shaving, on the few occasions I do purchase razors, I buy from a company called Dollar Shave Club.

The company burst onto the scene in 2012 with a memorable video of their CEO Michael Dubin describing, in a nonchalant and sarcastic manner, why their "Blades Are Fucking Great". Dollar Shave Club sells their razors online, offering a range of subscriptions to consumers.

At each stage of the order process, potential consumers are showered with positive affirmations. "The best thing you can put on your face", "great choice", "this will be life-changing", are just three examples. As consumers move through the conversion funnel, the messaging gets warmer and more self-satisfying. Dollar Shave Club has no problems flattering them.

Once the razors and shaving accessories arrive, many consumers will believe their skin has never felt softer, questioning why they ever spent more than $1 on razors previously. Consumers justify their purchases using the affirmations they were given with during the buying process, overlooking any negative issues they might have experienced.

We over-attribute positive features to products we've chosen and negative features to products not chosen.

High School Grades

Memories and our recollections of past events can be distorted by time, even for very significant events. Researchers wanted to examine our tendency to distort past events, hypothesising we often inflate them, or put another way, remember them better than they actually were (Bahrick et al., 1996).

One study examined the accuracy and distortion of memory using a group of first-year university students. The participants were asked to recall grades from all four years of high-school in five subject areas; mathematics, science, history, foreign language and English.

Researchers analysed the results by calculating an asymmetry ratio from 0 to 1. An asymmetry ratio of 0.5 indicated no distortion of grades, that is they recalled their grades perfectly. Ratios larger than 0.5 indication grade distortion upwards, and anything below 0.5 indicated grade distortion downwards.

High School Grades (Bahrick et al., 1996)

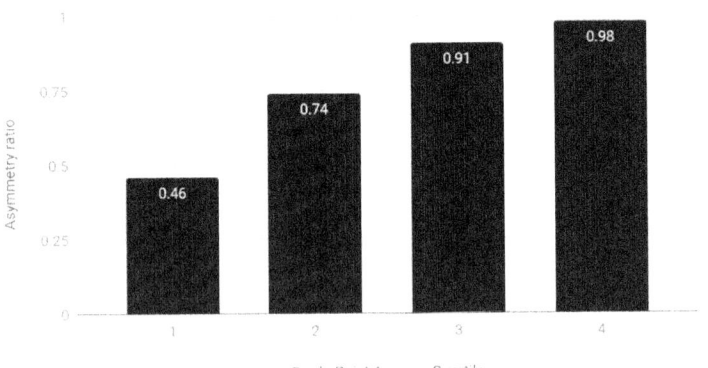

The accuracy of recall was fairly consistent across all grades. Surprisingly though, almost all those who achieved the highest grade point averages were most likely to distort their grades (M = 0.98) when compared to those in all the other quartiles (Q1 M = 0.46, Q2 M = 0.74, and Q3 M = 0.91).

In fact, distortion of grades dropped in line with the grade point average (Q4 = 0.98, Q3 M = 0.91, Q2 M = 0.74, and Q1 M = 0.46). Those in the bottom quartile for grade point average actually recalled slightly deflated grades.

Most participants inflated their actual high school grade, meaning that their distortions could be attributed to memory reconstructions in a positive and emotionally gratifying direction. It can be argued those in the top quartile were more competitive in academia and thus inflated their grades to a larger extent than those in the lower quartiles.

This experiment suggests that positive distortions can occur within a short time period. In a similar experiment, participants were asked to recall university grades fifty years after graduation. Researchers found participants again positively distorted their grades to a similar extent, and that the effect of positive distortion was greater for better students and for courses students enjoyed more (Bahrik et al., 2008).

Participants tended to remember their choices and experiences in a way that minimises regret and maximises satisfaction (see: choice paradox). Remembering the past as better is more emotionally gratifying than remembering foregone opportunities as better. When these choices and experiences are more important to us the effect is heightened.

Life Choices

Examining the choice-supportive bias in more detail a group of researchers gave participants various real-life scenarios in which they had to choose between two options; two job candidates, two potential blind dates, and two roommates (Mather et al., 2000).

In each scenario, researchers showed the participants a list of positive and negative attributes associated with each option to help participants make a decision. For example, in the roommate scenario, the negative features included; "leaves dirty laundry piled around the room" and positive features including; "good at resolving conflicts".

Participants were first asked to report their preference between the two options for each scenario. After each participant made their decision, they were shown a list of all the positive and negative features for both options and asked them to recall which feature belonged to which option in the various scenarios.

Researchers then analysed the responses using an asymmetry score. Essentially this was a calculation that showed whether a participant incorrectly recalled more positive features to their selection over the choice they rejected. Positive asymmetry scores indicated participants remembered more positive features for the option they had selected, whereas negative asymmetry scores indicated participants remembered more negative features for the option they had selected. An asymmetry score of 0 meant participants had associated all the features with the correct options.

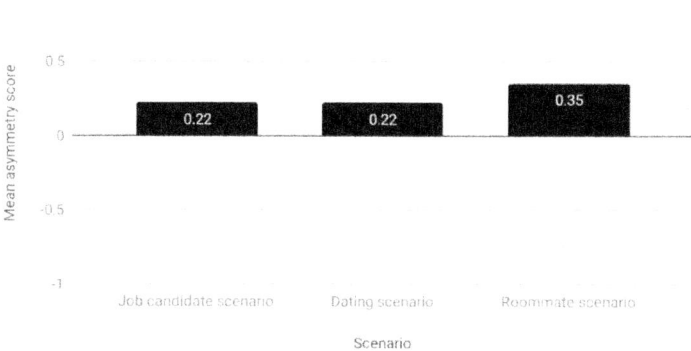

Life Choices (Mather et al., 2000)

For each of the three scenarios, the overall asymmetry score was significantly greater than 0 (M = 0.22 job candidate, M = 0.22 dating, and M = 0.35 roommate). Participants recalled far more positive features of their selections and in-turn more negative features to the items they had not selected.

We have a desire to stay true to commitments because they directly relate to our self-image (Cialdini, 2009). Participants attempted to rationalise any negative features observed to justify their choice made and protect their self-image.

Young and Old

In the previous experiment, participants were all undergraduate university students. Researchers wanted to test if the significance of our choice-supportive bias in different age groups (Mather & Johnson, 2000).

To do this they conducted a similar experiment, with one major difference, they selected participants from two age categories and split them into two groups; young adults age 18 - 26 years old and older adults aged 67 - 83 years old.

This time participants were given four scenarios, each with two options to choose from; two houses, two job candidates, two airline flights and two potential blind dates. As in the previous experiment, participants were shown a list of positive and negative features associated with both options to help them make a decision.

Participants were first asked to report their preference between the two options for each scenario. However, instead of asking participants to immediately recall the positive and negative features of each option in the various scenarios, they were asked to return two days later to perform the task.

The results were then processed using the same asymmetry score used in the previous experiment for analysis.

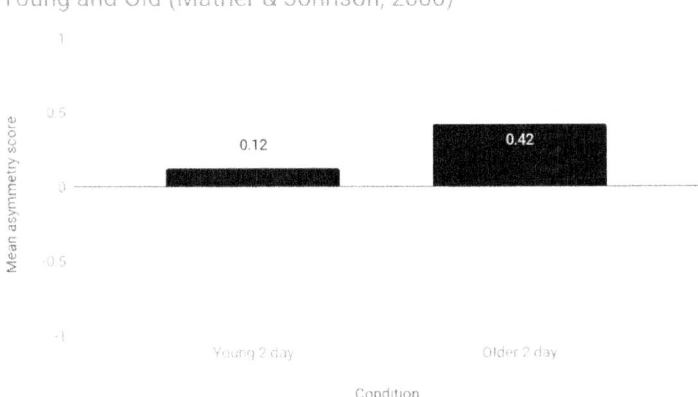

Young and Old (Mather & Johnson, 2000)

As seen previously, participants asymmetry scores were all, on average, greater than 0. The older group of participants recalled significantly more positive features to their selection (M = 0.42) than the participants in the younger age condition (M = 0.12).

The mean asymmetry score for the young participant condition (M = 0.12) was lower than all those calculated in the first, very similar experiment. This was somewhat expected given participants in this experiment waited two days before recalling features to the options they were presented with. Surprisingly, the older group saw a heightened choice-supportive bias after two days. The mean asymmetry score for this condition (M = 0.42) was higher than all asymmetry scores in the first experiment (M = 0.22 job candidate, M = 0.22 dating, and M = 0.35 roommate).

Older participants had a heightened choice-supportive memory remembering far more positive attributes from their choices than negative ones when compared to younger people.

Imaginary Memories

Our memories can be distorted for a range of reasons. We often try to "fill in the blanks" using social cues to aid us (see: social default bias) or by seeking out more information from other sources about why we made a decision. Though as demonstrated previously, we try to remember our decisions as the correct, looking for positive features in our choices (see: confirmation bias).

In a similar setup to the previous experiment, researches used five choice scenarios that each included two options.

roommates, summer internships, apartments, used cars, and potential dating partners (Henkel et al., 2007).

There were 10-12 features listed for each of the two options in a scenario. Each option included an equal number both positive and negative features. For example, in the used car scenario participants chose between a red and a black car, with positive attributes that included "high resale value" and negative attributes that included "mileage on odometer".

In each scenario, researchers asked participants to select their preferred option. Each participant then returned 2 days after making their selection to complete a memory test where they were asked to recall the option they had originally chosen and whether each feature was associated with the option they chose or had been associated with the option they rejected.

The results were then processed using the same asymmetry score used in the previous experiment for analysis.

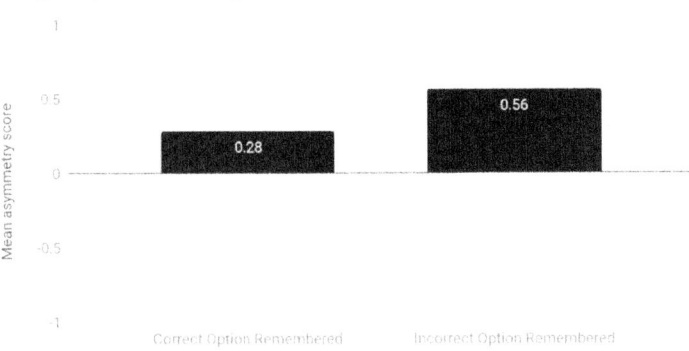

Imaginary Memories (Henkel & Mather, 2007)

When participants correctly remembered which option they had selected, asymmetry scores were significantly greater than zero (M = 0.28), and thus revealed a bias favouring chosen options as they attributed more positive features to them.

For the choices in which participants incorrectly remembered which option they originally chose, participants significantly favoured the options they thought they chose, rather than the ones they actually chose (M = 0.56). Participants attributed more positive features to the options they thought they chose and more negative features for the options they originally chose.

The average asymmetry score for those that recalled their choice incorrectly (M = 0.56) was significantly higher than those who correctly remember their original choice during recall (M = 0.28). These findings suggest that people who cannot remember their past decisions accurately try to fill gaps in their memory using the information available to them at the time (see: availability heuristic), often leading to an incorrect and more vivid recall.

When participants struggled to remember the reasoning as to why they made past choices, they tended to attribute a heightened level of positive features to their decisions (and negative features to the options they didn't choose) based on their beliefs at the time.

Product Gems

1. **Get consumers to commit early**
   Consumers have a desire to stay true to commitments because it directly relates to their self-image (Cialdini, 2009). We therefore attempt to rationalise any product problems seen, justify the choice made and protect our self-image. Try to leverage a consumers desire to be consistent by having consumers make an initial, small commitment, whether that's a verbal statement of intent or a small down-payment. Future requests can then be made that reinforce this initial commitment.

2. **Use positive affirmations**
   The big idea behind the choice-supportive bias is that people will try to convince themselves that they made the right decision. As demonstrated by Dollar Shave Club, reassuring consumers on the choices they make to enhance their own choice-supportive bias can result in greater post-purchase satisfaction. Online retailers could also show previously visited pages and previously purchased items to visitors (in other words remind consumers that they have already "chosen" you). *Example: Amazon.*

3. **Celebrate a user's 'correct' choice**
   When consumers make a decision, reward them with praise as this helps to reinforce their perception that they made the right choice. This could be done by popping a note in the purchase email telling consumers how much others also loved the product, giving applicable quotes and ratings, for instance. Such an experience will

soothe any post-purchase tension experienced, especially for more expensive orders.

4. **Solicit consumer reviews**

   As we desire our past choices to be rational and well-made, we're more likely to recommend or submit a positive review of a product purchased than a negative one. Consumers could be encouraged to share a review. This could be done by framing a review call-to-action to suggest that the product experience is indeed great and if they'd like to confirm that.

5. **Think about timing**

   When we struggle to recall the reasoning for a selection, we're more likely to attribute more positive features to it. If you're trying to solicit reviews for quickly consumed products or services, consider sending a prompt for consumers to leave feedback some weeks after the estimated consumption date.

6. **The effect is heightened for expensive products**

   The more we invest in something both monetary and emotionally the more likely consumers will refuse to admit, in light of any shortcomings experienced with the product, that their decision was made in poor judgement.

7. **Beware of younger consumers**

   The bias is less pronounced in younger people. If you target this generation, you will have to work harder to get consumers to believe they made the right choice when they experience any faults. This might explain why young people are less likely to be tied to brand names.

5. Centre-Stage Effect

When choosing from a set of products, we prefer the one in the middle

When products, people or other options are arranged vertically or horizontally, we tend to prefer the one placed in the middle.

In the UK, there was a popular game show called The Weakest Link broadcast on television that aired between 2000 and 2012. The show was presented by Anne Robinson who was known for her sharp and forthright style, to put it mildly.

If you're not familiar with the game, each contestant answered a question in a sequence determined by their position in a lineup. Each correct answer earned an ever-increasing sum of money until the pot was "banked" or kept, at which point the value of the pot was reset, but the round continued. At the end of each round, the contestants voted who they'd like to eliminate until one person, the winner, remained.

If players were acting rationally, they would vote out the "weakest link", the worst player, at the end of each round in order to "bank" the most money in preceding rounds. However, the number of incorrect answers given was not the only determining factor used by the players when deciding who to vote off.

In many cases, players overlooked errors that those in the centre of the line-up made to a greater extent than errors made by those in extreme positions. This gave centre position holders more favourable assessments and, as such, they were often ignored when it came to voting. During the twelve years that the show aired, significantly more winners came from the centre of the stage.

This phenomenon is known as the centre-stage effect, and we are influenced by it every single day. Positioning is vitally important and has drastic implications on consumer behaviour, and your own success.

Supermarket Shelves

Browsing the seemingly endless aisles stacked full of weird and wonderful products in my local supermarket, I find myself asking "Who buys all this stuff?" when trying to choose between twenty varieties of baked beans presented on the shelves.

When you're looking at items on a supermarket shelf, you are looking at the result of a planogram. A planogram is defined as a "diagram or model that indicates the placement of retail products on shelves in order to maximise sales".

Within these planograms, one phrase commonly used is "eye-level is buy-level", indicating that products positioned at eye level are likely to sell better. It's no accident that eye level is generally in the middle of the shelf—supermarket shelves are designed around this magic measurement. It is very likely you'll find that the more expensive options are placed at eye level or just below, while the store's own-brand products are placed higher or lower on the shelves.

Each one of those twenty baked bean varieties has been meticulously placed as a result of many hours of research. **Retailers know products are chosen more often when placed in the middle of an array and they use this to influence your purchase decisions and their bottom line.**

Next time you are in a supermarket, just keep note of how many times you need to bend down or stretch to find something you need.

Chewing Gum

Let's start by taking a look at a clear example of the effect in action; instances where people prefer the middle option in an array to options. In a controlled experiment forty-eight participants were shown three varieties of chewing gum: Spearmint, Peppermint and Winter Frost (Valenzuela & Raghubir, 2009). The packets were laid out in a line on the table and presented in varying orders to each of the participants.

Each participant was then asked which packet of chewing gum they would choose for themselves.

Chewing Gum (Valenzuela & Raghubir, 2009)

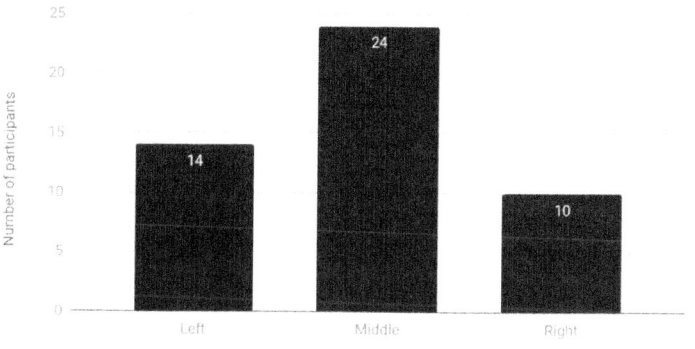

Chewing gum placement

The chewing gum variety placed in the middle was chosen half the time regardless of the variety (24/48), while the one on the left was chosen 29.17% of the time (14/48) and the one on the right chosen 20.83% of the time (10/48).

Participants significantly favoured the product in middle position in a line of similar products.

University Ratings

The chewing gum experiment not only identified a clear preference for the middle product, but there also seemed to be a slight preference for items placed on the left side of the table. Another set of researchers wanted to test this hypothesis.

In the experiment, 362 participants, all current students, were asked to complete a survey about their experience at the university by rating twenty-two positive statements (e.g. "My course has been enjoyable") on a 5-point Likert scale (Nicholls et al., 2007).

The participants were divided into two groups. One group answered using a 5-point Likert scale that ranged from 'definitely disagree' on the far left to 'definitely agree' on the far right (ascending scale). The other group answered using the same 5-point scale; however, for these participants, the scale ranged from 'definitely agree' on the far left to 'definitely disagree' on the far right (descending).

University Ratings (Nicholls et al., 2007)

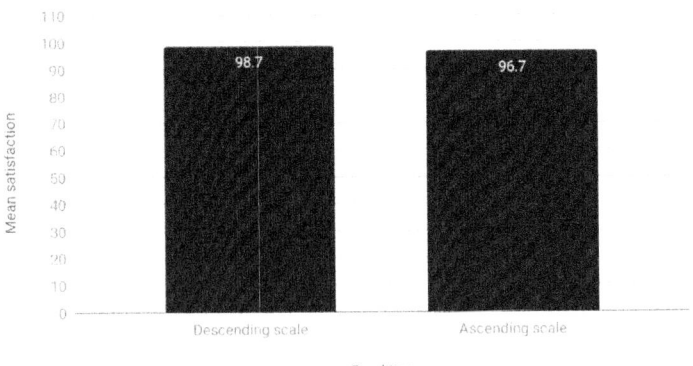

Out of a maximum score of 110 (5*22), an analysis revealed that overall satisfaction was slightly higher for those presented with the descending Likert scale that started on the left with 'definitely agree' (M = 98.7) than those shown the ascending scale (M = 96.7).

The students' natural bias for the left meant those answering using the descending Likert scale responded with 'definitely agree' to 27% more statements than the other group of students—that is, their views came out as more positive. By contrast, those students who answered using the ascending scale that began on the left with 'definitely disagree' responded more often with 'mostly disagree', meaning their views came out overall as more negative.

Generally, we prefer the middle option, but also have a natural leaning towards options placed on the left too.

Researchers attributed this to the way the brain works. Whatever the cause, this bias for the left is profound given the widespread use of questionnaires like this, from product reviews to academic research (including a large number in this book!). In fact, the questions used in this experiment were the same as those used by the Higher Education Funding Council for England in a survey of 250,000 students!

Pretzels (part 1)

As humans, we often focus our attention on the middle. We position our cars in the middle of a lane when driving, we place our computer screens in the middle of our view when working, we hang pieces of artwork in the middle of the wall. You get the idea. Researchers wanted to test if the centre-stage effect can be explained in terms of greater attention paid to the middle item.

In this experiment, the participants were shown a line of five different pretzel flavours all produced by the same brand (Valenzuela & Raghubir, 2009). Participants were told that each pretzel was the same price, $2.19. The order of pretzels in the line was randomised for each participant. Each participant was told they had been asked to choose one of the flavours to take to an upcoming party.

Participants were then asked to rank their preferences from 1 (favourite) to 5 (least favourite) for each pretzel. Finally, the participants were asked recall as many of the five flavours as possible.

Pretzels (Part 1) (Valenzuela & Raghubir, 2009)

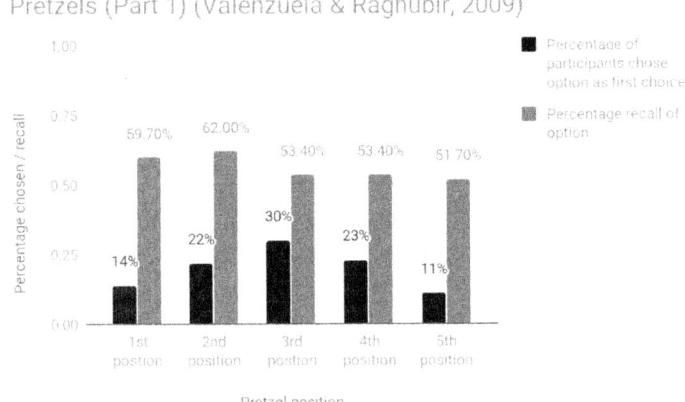

Participants ranked the variety in the centre as their first preference 30% of the time. There was a clear, normal distribution of participants' preference (M = 14, 22%, 30%, 23%, 11% for position 1-5). If participants were acting rationally, we would expect to see an even distribution of first choices across all conditions.

Perhaps surprisingly, there was no significant difference in the percentage of times a variety was recalled as a result of its position (M = 59.7%, 62.1%, 53.4%, 53.4%, 51.7% for position 1-5). While the variety in the middle position was chosen more as an option, it was recalled a similar amount of times as the options in other positions.

Again, there was a clear preference for the middle option as well as a slight preference for the furthest left option than the equivalent right option. However, preferences for central positions cannot be explained in terms of higher attention paid to those positions.

Pretzels (part 2)

Not all products in shops are laid out in a planogram. I sometimes shop at a bulk clothing retailer, TK Maxx, where the clothing rails appear to have no order—in fact, a level of disorder at times. It seems unlikely the centre-stage effect can influence when the position does not seem to be informative.

In this experiment, the scenario used was almost identical to part one, except this time nine varieties of pretzels were used instead of five (Valenzuela & Raghubir, 2009). Participants were split into two groups; half of the participants were told; "the presentation order had been selected at random" (random), while the other half were told that the presentation "represented real product placement by a local retailer" (retailer).

Participants were then asked to rank-order their preferences from 1 (favourite) to 7 (least favourite).

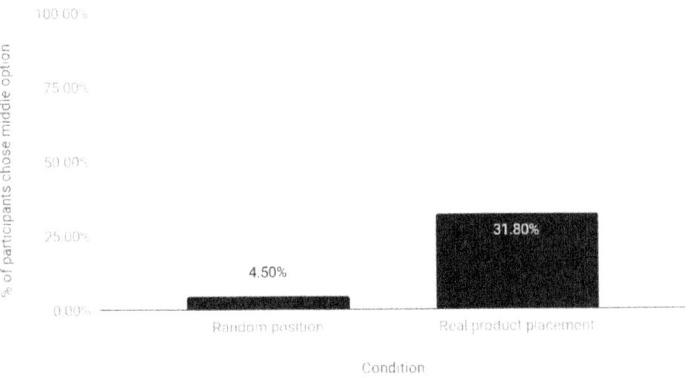

Pretzels (Part 2) (Valenzuela & Raghubir, 2009)

When participants believed there was a level of order in the options presented, that is the retailers had consciously organised their position, they ranked the middle option as their favourite 31.8% of the time. Astoundingly, the participants who believed the pretzels were in a completely random order chose the middle option just 4.5% of the time, well below the average odds of 11.1% (1/9).

The choice of the middle option was contingent on whether participants believed that the ordering of options was informative versus random. When the participants believed there was no clear order to the options presented, they did not gravitate towards the middle option—in fact, it appeared they actively avoided it.

Pretzels (part 3)

Our motivations for buying products for ourselves often differ from when buying for others. While I might choose an aesthetically pleasing watch for someone as a birthday present, when choosing for myself, I'm likely to select something more functional. Researchers also hypothesised the centre-stage effect could be greater when people are making purchases for others with relatively unknown preferences to their own.

The scenario used to test this was again the same as in part one, with participants shown five different pretzel varieties (Valenzuela & Raghubir, 2009). This time the participants were split in half. Half of the participants were told, "You are shopping for a party where guests need to bring a snack that everyone will like" (others), while the remaining participants were told, "You are shopping for a party where guests need to bring a snack that is their own personal favourite" (self).

All participants were asked to rate their purchase intentions for each pretzel for the party on a 7-point scale from 1 (Definitely will not purchase) to 7 (Definitely will purchase).

Pretzels (Part 3) (Valenzuela & Raghubir, 2009)

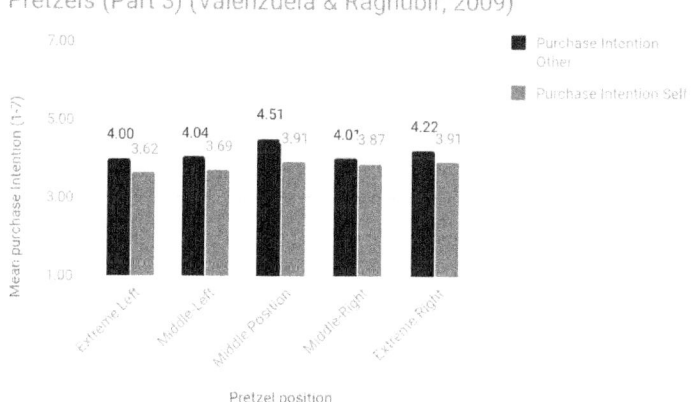

Out of a maximum score of 14, researchers found clear evidence of a centre-stage effect for those choosing for others (M = 4.00, 4.04, 4.51, 4.01, 4.22 for positions 1-5), but not for those choosing for themselves (M = 3.62, 3.69, 3.91, 3.87, 3.91 for position 1-5).

The results suggest that centre-stage effect being based on inferences of popularity. We are more likely to take popularity into account when purchasing on behalf of others whose preferences are not as well-known as our own.

The centre-stage effect is stronger when consumers are making purchase decisions for others rather than for themselves.

Socks

So far, we've looked at studies where options were placed horizontally. In many cases, options are presented vertically, and more often than not, vertically and horizontally. It was assumed by researchers that the centre-stage effect would be observed in vertical arrays too. However, as any good researcher would, they wanted to test this theory to be sure.

One hundred participants were shown a display of five identical pairs of white socks hung in a vertical line with each sock placed 17 cm apart (Rodway et al., 2012). The participants were split into two groups; one group was shown the display placed where the top was 171 cm above the ground (around eye level), while the other group saw a lower display with the top sock 99 cm above the ground (around thigh level).

Each participant was then asked to choose the pair of socks that they most preferred.

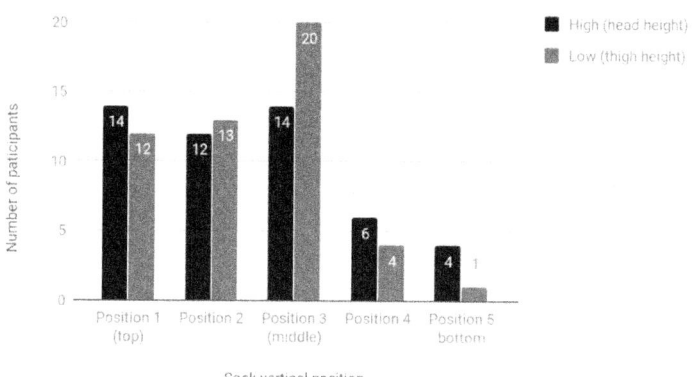

Socks (Rodway et al., 2012)

The centre-stage effect was observed in-line with expectations; the middle sock proved to be the most preferred in each display height, although much more so in the low display. It was selected as the favourite twenty and fourteen times for the low and high displays respectively.

Where the results get interesting, and something the researchers did not expect, was the significant reduction in preference for pairs of socks placed in the lowest two locations in both display heights, where they were selected as favourite six and four times for positions four and five in the high display and one and four times in the low display.

The results suggest that the relative height does not influence the centre-stage effect; rather, it is the position in the line-up that counts with a markedly reduced preference for options in the lowest positions.

Again, think about a supermarket. How many times do you reach for items on the bottom shelf?

Product Gems

1. **It's all about the middle**
   The centre-stage effect has strong implications for product positioning, such as on shelves, in magazines, online, etc. Many online retailers present grids of similar products to shoppers. This bias suggests that products located towards the middle of an array, vertically or horizontally, are generally be perceived as being more popular. It is therefore essential for your brand to ensure that it is your product enjoying the middle position, or as a retailer that the products you want to sell more of are placed centrally. This can be a powerful marketing strategy for new products or those you're struggling to sell.

2. **Keep it orderly**
   As part two of the pretzel experiment demonstrated, when consumers believe there is no logical order to the options presented, they will not be influenced by the centre-stage effect. For example, if a brand was trying to increase sales of a new version of their washing powder, placing it in the centre of an array of the other varieties of washing soap on offer has the potential to increase sales. However, a marketer must make sure that the other varieties are similar overall with only one or two distinctions to make the array appear well-thought-out. In the case of washing powder, this could be achieved by placing a product with a new scent in the middle of two existing scents.

3. **Be explicit to minimise the effect**
   Consumers often gravitate towards the middle option because it is assumed to be more popular among the general population. When the most

popular option is explicitly stated, perhaps in a bestseller list, the belief that the middle option is the most popular disappears, as does the effect. Similarly, for digital products and marketplaces, providing users with the functionality to sort products by popularity will have the same effect.

4. **Opportunity for extra revenue streams**
This bias also has strong implications for brands that advertise digitally. It suggests that advertisers can charge brands a premium for ensuring that their products take the central position online. This may be particularly true for sites such as Amazon that display a vast variety of products in both vertical and horizontal arrays.

5. **The gift-buyer booster**
As the bias is found to be stronger when consumers are shopping for others, identifying exactly when consumers are in this state, and for what items they are likely to be in this state, can help marketers capitalise on this bias. For example, this bias can be used by gift and party shops selling different brands of products.

6. **Use beyond product placement**
The centre-stage effect is observed in a wide range of situations, including consumers responding to questionnaires, selecting a member of a team, or when choosing political candidates during television debates.

7. **Use other biases to further enhance the effects**
The persuasive nature of the centre-stage effect can be increased if it is combined with social proof. Software-as-a-service (SaaS) providers do this very well by not only placing their most profitable plan

centrally on their website but by also highlighting it as their "most popular" plan.

8. **Think about product feedback questionnaires carefully**
   Likert 5-point scales are regularly used in product assessments (e.g., "On a scale of 1 to 5, how did we do?"). As we've seen, the orientation of options on a scale can have a big impact on which options are selected with respondents generally having a left-leaning bias. Randomising the order of the scale for each respondent or using a mix of positive and negative questions can minimise the influence of this left-leaning bias.

6. Status Quo Bias

We prefer to do nothing and keep things the way they are or stick with a decision made previously

Across a range of everyday decisions, such as whether to move houses, trade in a car, or even whether to change the TV channel, there is a considerable tendency to maintain the status quo and refrain from acting.

The first 90 minutes of my weekdays are usually exactly the same. Every day I wake up at 7 a.m., then 60 minutes of yoga, followed by a nice long breakfast, a bowl of porridge and a glass of hot water with lemon.

Some people call me boring. Maybe I am. Though I'm not really boring. A few years ago, I switched from adding a banana, my favoured porridge topping for the previous four years, to blueberries. Once I had made the switch, I never got around to going back to bananas and have since stuck with blueberries.

The thought of changing porridge for eggs sounds nice, as does going for a run instead of my yoga practice. Time and time again, I pass up these options in favour of the status quo. Deep down I know I'm missing out; all those other breakfast options look incredibly tasty, but there's something that's subconsciously got me stuck in my ways.

Many of us resist change in all areas of our lives, not just breakfast. You might have a favourite restaurant you regularly visit, at which you have a favourite menu option that you always order. You eat it at your favourite table, and once the meal is complete, you tip the same amount to the waiting staff as you always do, regardless of the service on that particular day.

Even when we know the status quo is not beneficial, we often find it hard to overcome the natural urge to stay on the same path. Perhaps that meal option at your favourite restaurant is incredibly unhealthy and is causing you to gain weight.

The status quo bias is pervasive in both inconsequential and major decisions. Oftentimes we are held back by what we believe to be the safe option, simply because it is the default, as reflected in the old adage, "when in doubt, do nothing".

Power Supply

When was the last time you changed utility provider? We all know cheaper gas, electricity, telephone, TV, internet, or insurance packages are out there, but we rarely switch to them for a whole range of "good" reasons. Perhaps you don't have time. Perhaps you don't want to be tied into a contract. Perhaps the service won't be as reliable. Perhaps something will go wrong during the switchover. For most of us, these shouldn't be big enough concerns not to make large savings on our monthly bills.

In California, 2200 customers of a large utility provider, Pacific Gas & Electric, were asked about their preferences regarding trade-offs between service reliability and rates. For those who had poor service, namely regular power outages, 58% opted to remain with the same provider, even when the alternatives offered a more reliable service at only a slightly higher monthly cost. Conversely, 60% of those already paying more for the high-reliability provider were unwilling to switch to the cheaper, slightly less reliable providers, even if they offered significant monthly savings!

It is only when gas and electricity prices are significantly increased, as happens regularly in the UK, do consumers decide to make a switch (although, even then, many still choose to do nothing). We tend to avoid change unless the incentive to do so is compelling.

Investing Inheritance

Financial products, like utilities, can often be incredibly confusing. It's not unusual for someone to remain with the same bank or credit card provider for their entire lives. A group of Harvard researchers conducted an experiment to test for status quo effects during financial investment decisions.

The 116 participants were split into three groups (Samuelson & Zeckhauser, 1988). One group was told they had recently inherited some money from their great uncle and were considering investing it in the stock of a moderate-risk company (30% chance of profit, 20% chance of loss) and a high-risk company (40% chance of profit, 40% chance of loss) (no status quo).

The other two groups were given a similar scenario with a slight twist. In these two groups, participants were told they had not only inherited money but also inherited stocks in a company. One group were told the stocks were in the moderate-risk company (moderate-risk status quo) while the others were told it was for the high-risk company (high-risk status quo).

All three groups were then asked which of the two companies' stocks they would like to invest their recently inherited money in.

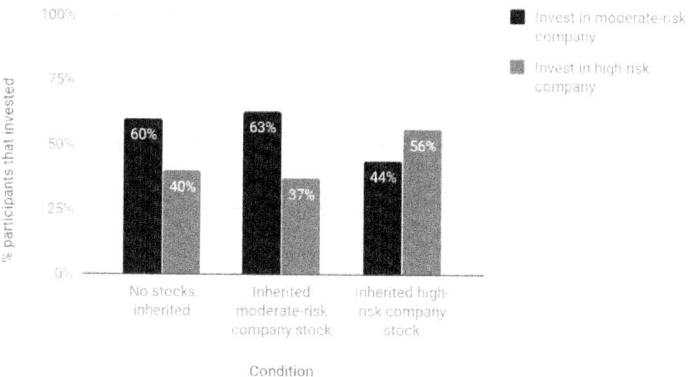

Investing Inheritance (Samuelson & Zeckhauser, 1988)

As expected, because of our inherent risk-averse nature, 60% of the participants in the group that only inherited money (and no stocks) were more likely to invest their new-found wealth in the moderate-risk company, compared to 40% who chose the high-risk company.

Those participants who inherited stocks in the moderate-risk company in addition to money were also more likely to invest the money in even more stock of the moderate-risk company (63%) rather than hedge their investments by placing the money in the new high-risk option (37%). The opposite outcome was observed in those who inherited the high-risk stock. These participants preferred to invest the inherited money in more of the high-risk stick (56%) than the moderate-risk stock (44%).

In both cases, those who inherited stocks were acting irrationally—most seasoned investors will tell you placing all your eggs in one basket is risky as any company can fail. In part, this behaviour can be attributed to the fact the participants were endowed with the stocks (see: endowment effect). However, both groups of participants still had an investment choice without forgoing existing stocks in either of the companies.

We tend to opt for the status quo in circumstances where we have a lack of understanding of the choices available, often leading us to make suboptimal decisions.

Highway Safety

Taxes; oh, how we loathe them. Especially when governments appear to waste our hard-earned money. Local governments commonly engage with local residents regarding decisions that will affect them. The status quo bias would suggest this is generally a bad idea because we prefer things in their current state, rather than the proposed, often improved, alternatives.

Examining this, eighty-four participants were asked to choose how they thought the US National Highway Safety Commission should spend its budget between two safety research programs (Samuelson & Zeckhauser, 1988). One program was aimed at improving car safety (promoting seat belts, improved bodywork, etc.), while the alternative focused on highway safety (building guardrails, setting new speed limits, etc.).

The participants were told that currently, 30% of the Commission's budget went towards car safety, with the remaining 70% spent on highway safety (highway safety status quo). They were then told the Commission was reassessing the allocation of funds for the following year. Participants were asked to consider the following two options and record their preference for how the funds should be allocated:

a) Allocate 70% to car safety and 30% to highway safety
b) Allocate 30% to car safety and 70% to highway safety

Highway Safety (Samuelson & Zeckhauser, 1988)

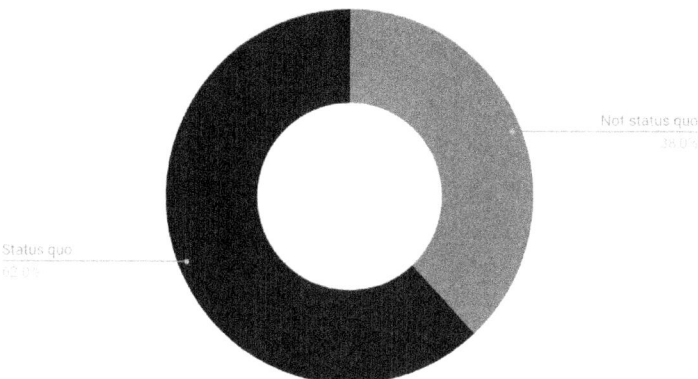

The majority of the participants, 62%, opted for the status quo or allocating 30% to car safety and 70% to highway safety. Only 38% preferred the option against the status quo to increase the car safety budget.

Even for decisions that did not immediately or clearly have an impact on their lives, or put another way, when the individual risk of change was low, participants still opted for the status quo.

Car Colour

Many of the examples and studies raised in this book consider car sales; I admit I do have a fondness for them. However, they prove brilliant examples because it is very likely you have purchased a car and, as a result, have probably fallen victim to at least one bias during the process.

Take another experiment; 202 participants were told they had placed themselves on the waiting list at a Volvo dealer to order a new car that was in high demand (Samuelson & Zeckhauser, 1988). Each participant was told that to speed up delivery they had agreed to accept any of the four colours the cars came in: red, blue, tan, or white.

Participants were then split into three groups. The first group was told that two days ago, all four colours of the car had arrived, and they could choose any of the options (no status quo). The second group was told the dealer called two days ago to let them know a red car was in stock, however, when they arrived at the dealership, they found that the three other colours of the car had just been delivered and that they were free to change their mind to another colour instead (red status quo). The third group was told the dealer had called them two days ago to let them know the blue, tan, or white colours of the car had arrived and asked them to choose their preference. This group was then told, when arriving at the dealership, that the red car had also been unexpectedly delivered, and they could opt to choose it over their previous selection should they want to (other status quo).

After being told this information, the three groups of participants were then asked to choose which colour of car they finally wanted.

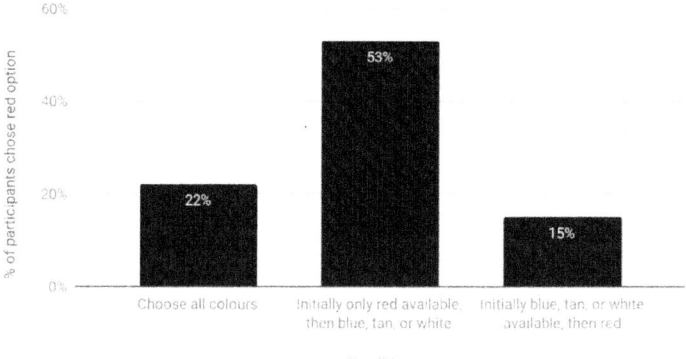

Car Colour (Samuelson & Zeckhauser, 1988)

When given the option of all four colours, 22% of participants opted for red. When participants had selected the red car in advance, 53% of them stuck with their decision when given the choice of the other three colours. However, just 15% of those who first chose either the blue, tan or white versions of the car subsequently changed their mind and opted for the red alternative when given a chance.

If these participants were acting rationally, we could expect them to select the red car a similar number of the times across all conditions. The same experiment was performed using the three other colours. In each version, the researchers found the same pattern of results.

Even when there is low effort and risk involved in changing our minds, our past decisions appear to heavily influence our future preferences in favour of the status quo.

Aeroplane Leases

The status quo bias works against us in our personal and professional lives. Critical decisions to a business' success can be hindered by our preference to maintain the norm, leading to stagnation and ultimately failure.

Twenty-eight senior managers of regional airlines were asked to consider a typical scenario for leasing new aircraft for two years (Samuelson & Zeckhauser, 1988). The participants were told that a strong economic forecast was predicted in year one of the lease because of high demand and stable airfares.

They were then given two leasing options to choose from; either six 100-seat aircraft (small fleet) or six 100-seat aircraft and four 150-seat aircraft (large fleet). In line with common leasing contracts, the participants were told they would have the option to change their decision in favour of the other at the end of year one should they wish.

Participants were then told that forecasts for year two were looking significantly worse, with lower demand and competitive price wars. They were then asked to select which combination of aircraft they would choose based on this information for the second year of the lease.

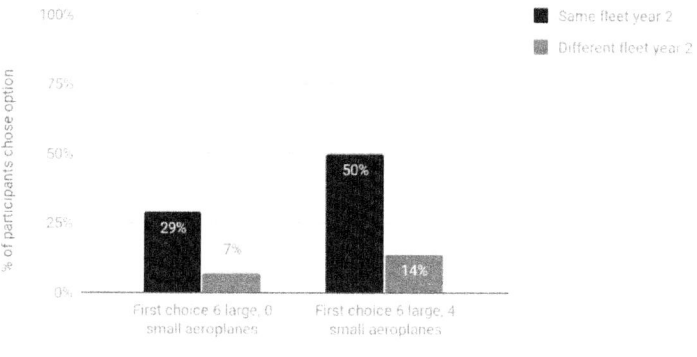

Aeroplane Leases (Samuelson & Zeckhauser, 1988)

The 36% of senior managers who first selected the smaller fleet option for year one were much more likely to keep the smaller fleet in year two. Of the 64% of senior managers who opted for the larger fleet during the first year, most of them decided to stick with their first option, to keep the larger fleet in year two.

This appears illogical. In bad economic conditions, we would expect most of the senior managers to opt for the smaller fleet size given there was no direct cost to change leases. Not only does the status quo bias cause us to unfairly overweight the losses for change, but more importantly, it causes us to ignore the opportunity cost of staying the same.

Car Insurance

In a final, real-life example, consider car insurance. In the early 1990s, citizens in the US states of New Jersey and Pennsylvania were offered two options for car insurance: an expensive option giving them full right to sue and a less expensive option with restricted rights to sue.

Critically, the default option was different for each state. Car owners in New Jersey were automatically given the limited right unless they made an active decision to opt to receive the full rights. In Pennsylvania, the default option was for the full rights to sue.

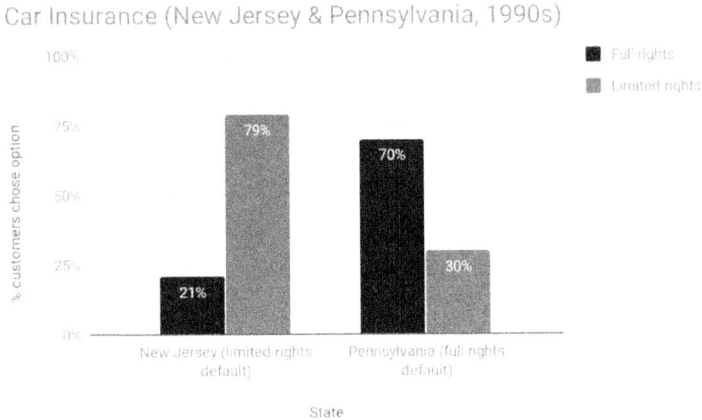

Car Insurance (New Jersey & Pennsylvania, 1990s)

During the 1990s, around 79% of New Jersey drivers had insurance policies with the limited right to sue, whereas 70% of Pennsylvania drivers had the full right to sue. Citizens of both states preferred the default option, the status quo. Astoundingly, the difference in amount spent on insurance premiums between the two states was about $200 million!

Organ donations rates around the world are another good example. In Austria, 99% of the population are registered to donate their organs after death. Only 4% of the people in Denmark are registered to donate. The difference? Austrian citizens are automatically enrolled to donate, whereas Danish citizens have to choose to opt-in to donate their organs after death.

We prefer the option with less effort when faced with a range of choices with no clear or compelling "right" choice.

Product Gems

1. **Balance the sense of risk**

   As the status quo bias has demonstrated, we often prefer the norm. This is because the perceived risk of change creates a fear of the unknown and anticipated regret. Once the risk of the status quo is greater than the risk of change, people will fully appreciate the value of the alternatives.

2. **Influence the status quo**

   Think about really compelling and clear messaging for potential customers to seriously consider a switch to your alternative. You can do this by setting a status quo, or baseline. Many service providers might provide information about the "average" quality consumers should expect. Take an internet service provider offering high-speed connections; they might advertise their recommended connection speeds other consumers required for streaming video—speeds that will likely align perfectly with the plans they offer.

3. **But be objective**

   Use third-party research to influence the status quo where possible. Customers would much rather hear from an objective party than your own biased opinions. Showing them how they are operating sub-optimally using respected and objective research will be much better received. Alternatively, "reference customers" who have recently switched to your product from a competitor can help set the perceived status quo in your favour.

4. **Consider transition costs**

   Companies that completely eliminate the behaviour change that product innovations require can help minimise the effects of the status quo bias. Toyota embraced this tactic with its hybrid electric vehicles, like the Prius. The Prius provides drivers with both the traditional internal-combustion engine and an innovative, self-charging electric engine. Tesla, with its highly innovative, all-electric Model 3 took the opposite approach, and so has taken much longer to reach mass-market appeal.

5. **Or Remove Them Entirely**
   Alternatively, if you're trying to get users to upgrade urgently, consider completely removing the old product entirely. Beware though, taking away the status quo can upset existing customers.

6. **Think about product enhancements carefully**
   Innovation is typically a good thing, though your existing consumers who know and love your product in its current state might not think the same way. Take Facebook as an example; over the past ten years, they have overhauled the user interface of the product a number of times. On each roll-out, a significant number of users complain that they don't like the new version, and "preferred the old one much better". To minimise the negative impact such changes might have on your customers, try to warn them in advance of pending alterations and the benefits they'll bring. If changes are more complex, consider a way to educate and guide users to speed up their understanding.

7. **Strive for 10x improvement**
   Another approach to managing customer resistance is for companies to make the relative benefits of their innovations so great that they overcome the consumers' overweighting of potential losses.

8. **Find early adopters**

   Another option is to seek out consumers who prize the benefits they could gain from a new product or only lightly value those they would have to give up for an existing product. In the case of electric vehicles, for instance, Toyota targeted environmentally conscious consumers. Less obviously, they could have also targeted consumers for whom access to petrol stations is a problem.

9. **Opt-in over opt-out**

   Having customers opt-in by default will increase uptake of the option as demonstrated in the car insurance experiment. The opt-out strategy can also be a useful tool to influence business decisions. For example, when proposing a new idea, make it clear that if senior management, or whoever is appropriate, doesn't intervene by a certain date, you will start to work on it. In other words, give them an "opt-out" decision to make instead of an "opt-in" one.

10. **Beware of stagnation**

    The status quo can cause research and development budgets to shrink as companies focus on replicating what is already working well. The fact is, most areas of business can find improvements, and you should be actively looking for them. That might be the products you offer, how you train staff, or even the food you place in the vending machines!

7. Social Default Bias

When we can't make informed decisions, we simply copy others' choices

When we're deciding between products but aren't well-informed, observing others' choices significantly influences our own decision. This leads to the creation of a powerful social default choice.

Three hundred yoga mats on Amazon. That's excluding colour variations. PVC or memory foam, thick or thin, organic or non-organic, the options are endless. The prices are too. Starting at £10 and increasing to as much as £100 for what look to be identical products.

Having recently turned to the online retailer when buying a present for a friend, I now feel like an expert on yoga mats.

With such a diverse array of options on offer, as product reviewers were keen to note, deciding upon which one to gift initially appeared a daunting task. That was until I realised many of these reviewers continually referenced a brand of yoga mat, Manduka.

"This mat is OK, but my friends Manduka mat is better", commented one reviewer, on another brands mat. "Should have spent the extra £20 for the Manduka" commented another. Three similar reviews later and I was sold, it had to be a Manduka mat.

Ignoring those that are able to think up gifts for friends, family, and seemingly, strangers with ease, many of us find buying presents for others a difficult task. One made only more difficult when we know very little about the type of presents we intend to buy. In these situations, we turn to others -- industry experts, existing product owners, marketing materials -- to influence the choices we make.

In fact, Nielsen reports that the most meaningful form of advertising is recommendations from friends and family: 83% of consumers in 60 countries say they trust these recommendations over any other form of advertising.

When our brains make decisions, it looks for cues. The strongest of those cues is to see what everyone else is doing. Social proof, or the social default, is one of the most powerful drivers of our everyday behaviour.

Beats

From Beyoncé to Kylie Jenner, celebrities now have a direct medium to their fan-base using social media. A single post can command thousands of "likes" from avid followers, and in-turn thousands of dollars for the social media influencers.

In six years, Interscope records mogul Jimmy Iovine and hip-hop icon Dr Dre turned Beats by Dr Dre headphones into a $1 billion-plus business. Beats control some 70 percent of the headphones market, thanks to lightning-fast marketing and a smart grasp of pop culture. The success of the company can, in large part, be attributed to Iovine's efforts to get celebrities photographed wearing the headphones on Instagram.

If you thought the endless product placement in music video after music video was tacky and tiresome, you weren't alone. "There would be times where we would be shooting a video until like six in the morning, and we had to do one more take with me or somebody in the video wearing some goddamn [Beats] headphones," Eminem exclaims. "Are you fucking kidding me?!"

Though clearly, it worked.

Getting an endorsement from a celebrity or social media influencer is a fantastic way to build brand credibility and convert more prospects. Consumers trust celebrities and influencers. If a celebrity is willing to put their neck out to endorse your product, it can increase a consumers confidence in a purchase.

Changing Towels (part 1)

If you've stayed at a major hotel, you've probably seen a little card in your room asking you to reuse your towels to help save the environment. One experiment aimed to test the effectiveness of these cards when social proof was used in the messaging (Cialdini et al., 2008).

Over an 80-day span, researchers collected data about towel reuse in 190 rooms in a mid-sized, mid-priced hotel in the United States. The guests were not aware that they were participants in the study.

Two different messages urging guests' participation in the towel reuse program were printed on signs positioned on washroom towel racks.

1. No social norm: One group of guests were shown messages printed on cards that read; "HELP SAVE THE ENVIRONMENT. You can show your respect for nature and help save the environment by reusing your towels during your stay".
2. Social norm: The second group had a card in their room that read; "JOIN YOUR FELLOW GUESTS IN HELPING TO SAVE THE ENVIRONMENT. Almost 75% of guests who are asked to participate in our new resource savings program do help by using their towels more than once".

Below each of the respective messages was instructions informing the guests how to indicate their willingness to participate in the program. The instructions stated, "If you choose to participate in the program, please drape used towels over the curtain rod or the towel rack. If you choose not to participate in the program, please place the towels on the floor."

Changing Towels (part 1) (Cialdini et al., 2008)

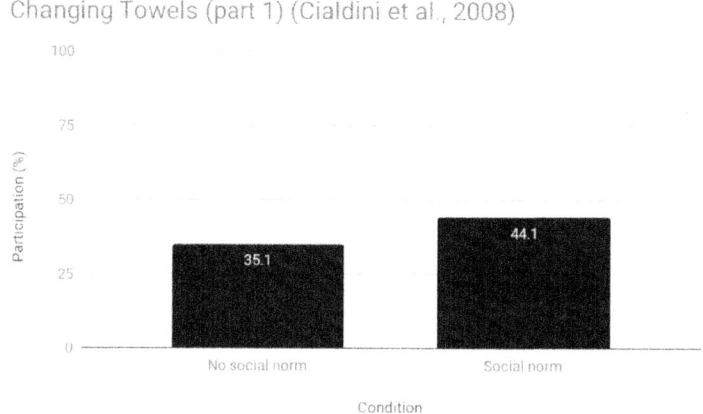

The message containing the social default, that almost 75% of other guests used their towels more than once, saw 44.1% of those that read the message do the same compared to just 35.1% who did the same when the message contained no social norm.

Hotel guests were especially motivated to reuse their towels when they learned that most others had chosen to participate in the environmental conservation program when compared to those who had no understanding of the social norms.

Changing Towels (part 2)

In experiment one, the social norm broadly referenced all other hotel guests. The researchers wanted to test whether they could increase engagement by changing the group used to define the social norm.

Several factors are known to influence the extent to which individuals will adhere to the descriptive norms of a given reference group. One important variable affecting the likelihood of norm adherence is the level of perceived similarity among others and a given individual (Burnkrant & Cousineau, 1975) -- people often evaluate themselves by comparing themselves to others, especially to others with whom they share similar personal characteristics.

A similar follow-up experiment conducted over 53 days examined towel reuse at the same hotel (Cialdini et al., 2008). In this experiment five variations of the message were printed on each card:

1. No social norm: The standard environmental message focused guests on the importance of environmental protection but did not provide any descriptive normative information: "HELP SAVE THE ENVIRONMENT. You can show your respect for nature and help save the environment by reusing your towels during your stay".

2. All guest norm: The guest identity descriptive norm message stated "JOIN YOUR FELLOW GUESTS IN HELPING TO SAVE THE ENVIRONMENT. In a study conducted in Fall 2003, 75% of the guests participated in our new resource savings program by using their towels more than once. You can join your fellow guests in this program to help save the environment by reusing your towels during your stay".

3. Same room norm: The message for the same room identity descriptive norm message stated "JOIN YOUR FELLOW GUESTS IN HELPING TO SAVE THE ENVIRONMENT. In a study conducted in Fall

2003, 75% of the guests who stayed in this room (#xxx) participated in our new resource savings program by using their towels more than once. You can join your fellow guests in this program to help save the environment by reusing your towels during your stay". Note that "(#xxx)" would be replaced with "(#313)" for room 313, for example.

4. All citizens norm: The citizen identity descriptive norm message stated "JOIN YOUR FELLOW CITIZENS IN HELPING TO SAVE THE ENVIRONMENT. In a study conducted in Fall 2003, 75% of the guests participated in our new resource savings program by using their towels more than once. You can join your fellow citizens in this program to help save the environment by reusing your towels during your stay".

5. Gender identity norm: The message for the gender identity descriptive norm condition stated "JOIN THE MEN AND WOMEN WHO ARE HELPING TO SAVE THE ENVIRONMENT. In a study conducted in Fall 2003, 76% of the women and 74% of the men participated in our new resource savings program by using their towels more than once. You can join the other men and women in this program to help save the environment by reusing your towels during your stay".

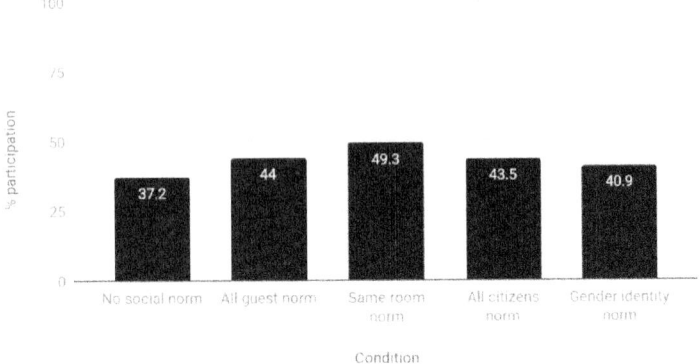

Changing Towels (part 2) (Cialdini et al., 2008)

% participation / Condition

No social norm: 37.2
All guest norm: 44
Same room norm: 49.3
All citizens norm: 43.5
Gender identity norm: 40.9

The same room identity descriptive norm condition yielded a significantly higher towel reuse rate (49.3%) than the other three descriptive norm conditions. When no social norm was mentioned, towel reuse was significantly lower (37.2%).

These results might prove initially surprising -- the same room messaging that produced the highest level of participation referenced the least meaningful norms of all the descriptive norm conditions. This messaging did not map to the individual's social identity but did map to the setting those individuals were currently occupying.

Existing research suggests the social default should map closely to an individual's social identity. Experiment two confirmed that individuals are also influenced by descriptive norms when the setting in which those norms are formed is comparable to the setting those individuals are currently occupying.

Tea Chooser (part 1)

When we're deciding between products but aren't well-informed, observing others' choices significantly influences our own decision, as clearly demonstrated by the yoga mat example.

In one experiment, non-Korean speaking participants were asked to observe a native Korean speaker make a selection from two brands of Korean tea (with packaging all in Korean, meaning participants would be pretty uninformed about which brand to go for) (Eun Huh et al., 2014).

The participants were split into two groups:

1. Public selection: Observed the tea-chooser select a tea before being asked to select one themselves. The tea-chooser remained in the room for the first group of participants.
2. Private selection: Observed the tea-chooser select a tea before being asked to select one themselves. The tea-chooser left the room for the first group of participants.

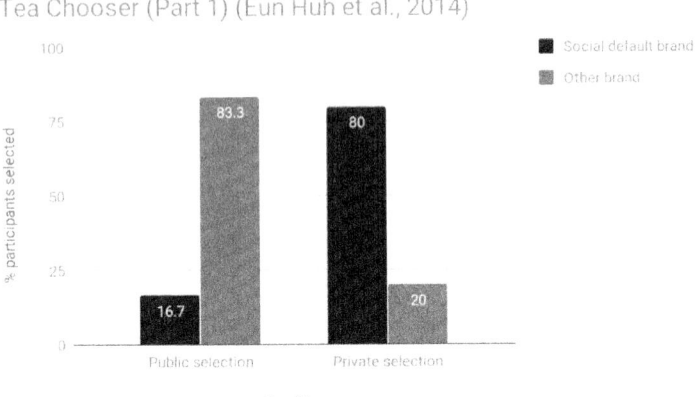
Tea Chooser (Part 1) (Eun Huh et al., 2014)

The two groups opted for completely different selections. When selecting in public, participants favoured the tea opposite to the one the tea-chooser selected (83.3%). However, when selecting in private, participants favoured the social default brand selected by the tea-chooser (80%).

Interestingly, these results contradict most common findings in social psychology, which themselves suggest that we're more likely to imitate others' behaviour in public (Deutsch & Gerard, 1955).

Participants were found to be much more likely to choose the same tea bag as that selected by the chooser (social default). Crucially, this was only when the chooser was not present in the room when the choice was being made.

Cracker Chooser

If choice imitation occurs as a result of deliberate informational influence, higher stakes should lead to more imitation, as participants should be more likely to use information gleaned from the observed choice in a high-stakes decision (Baron et al., 1996).

A second experiment introduced choice imitation as a result of deliberate informational influence by having some participants consume their choice (Eun Huh et al., 2014). Again, non-Korean speaking participants were asked to select their preference, this time from two different types of Korean crackers, both labelled in Korean.

As before, participants watched a native Korean speaker first make a selection from the two options. However, in this experiment, the groups were split into two groups based on the stakes involved in their decision.

1. Low stake condition: Participants were told that they could take their choice of crackers home with them as remuneration for participating in the study.
2. High stake condition: Participants were told that they had to eat their choice of crackers during the experimental session.

All participants were then asked which cracker brand they preferred.

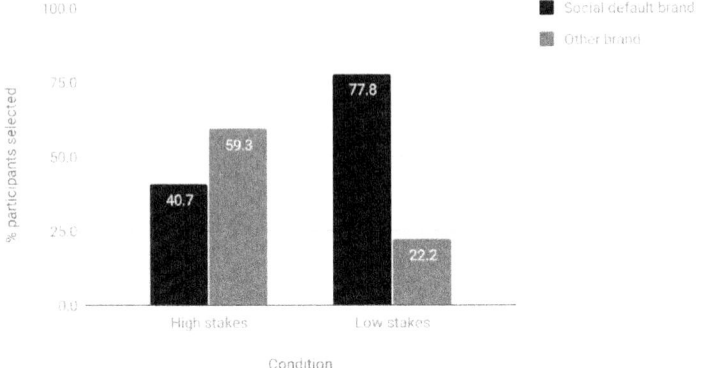

Cracker Chooser (Eun Huh, Vosgerau & Morewedge, 2014)

When facing a low-stakes decision, when they were given the crackers to take home, participants chose the same crackers the cracker-chooser selected (77.9%), the social default. Participants were less likely to mimic the cracker-choosers selection when making a high-stakes decision -- having to eat the crackers that they chose (59.3%).

Social defaults engendered choice mimicry for a low-stake but not a high-stakes decision. Considering the Amazon gift buying example, the results indicate that we're more likely to follow social defaults when choosing for others or for commodity products.

Tea Chooser (part 2)

Traditions transcend communities, nationalities and cultures. Anyone who has travelled extensively will realise that many countries have completely different ways of doing things, processes that seem completely abnormal to that of your home country.

A follow up to the first tea choosing experiment tested whether social defaults, like traditional defaults, are more likely to engender choice mimicry when preferences are uncertain.

The procedure of this experiment was similar to Tea Chooser (part 1), however, two English brands of tea were introduced as choices in addition to the two Korean options used previously (Eun Huh et al., 2014).

The participants were split into two groups again and exposed to two slightly different scenarios:

1. Watched chooser: Participants observed a native Korean speaker choose one English breakfast tea and one Korean tea. After the tea-chooser had left the room participants were then asked to choose two teas, one Korean and one English out of the four, for themselves.
2. Did not watch chooser: Participants in this condition did not observe the native Korean making their choice before being asked to choose two teas, one Korean and one English out of the four, for themselves.

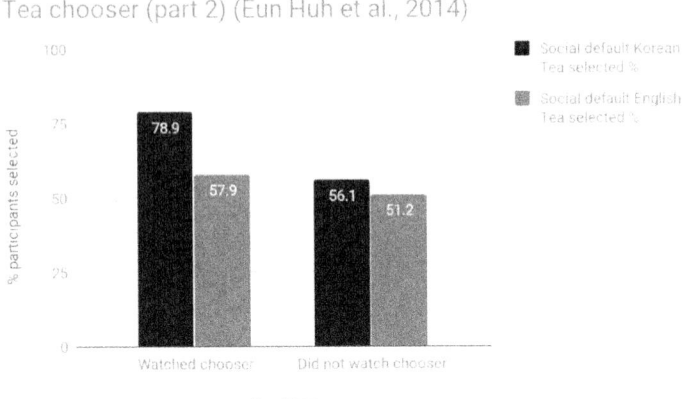

Tea chooser (part 2) (Eun Huh et al., 2014)

Participants were more likely to mimic the observed choice of the native Korean speaker when choosing from products of uncertain quality and flavour (i.e., Korean teas) (78.9%). Choice mimicry was less likely when choosing from products of more certain quality and flavour (English teas) (57.9%). Adding English text to the packaging made participants less likely to mimic the chooser.

Social defaults are less likely to occur when the person has information about a given situation, and if they already have a strong existing preference for a given product or brand. When we feel strongly about something, we're less likely to be swayed by external influences.

Product Gems

1. **Make it appropriate**
   The setting and context of the social default is important. Individuals are also influenced by descriptive norms when the setting in which those norms are formed is comparable to the setting those individuals are currently occupying.

2. **Works best in private**
   The social default effect is most likely to occur in private. Marketing messages based on social norms often work best when they reach a consumer in a private context, for example via email marketing or using flyers sent to their homes. This makes the effect particularly important for online retailers to consider the impact of social defaults, through product reviews or best-selling categories, for example.

3. **Limited product knowledge enhances the effect**
   The effect works best in industries where the choice is high, but our knowledge is relatively low. Wine is a great example. The effect may have the strongest effect for new product lines or/ industries (e-cigarettes, for example) too, where there is limited knowledge or launching an existing product in a new country, where local knowledge of an existing product or range is low.

4. **Has a greater influence on important decisions**
   Social defaults engendered choice mimicry for a low-stake but not a high-stakes decision. Those who are selling products or services that are traditionally gifted can leverage the effect to greater effect than those who sell products directly to consumers.

5. **Beware of brand preference**
   If you're using this technique, pick a target audience whom you think don't have a strong preference for your brand or your competitors, and are indifferent about which brand of the given product they use, as social defaults provide a powerful way to divert them towards your brand.
6. **Beware negative social proof**
   Negative social proof is the inadvertent misuse of the bias. It's when social proof is used in such a way that it has the opposite effect to that intended. For example, park rangers who suffered from the theft of wood placed signs reading; "Your heritage is being vandalised every day by theft losses of petrified wood of 14 tons a year, mostly a small piece at a time" (Cialdini et al., 2006). Since they emphasised the number of thieves, the psychologists worried they encouraged more stealing. They were right. Many social marketing campaigns still shock people with similarly daunting figures about the scale of the problem they're trying to solve which often significantly reduces the effectiveness of the campaign.

8. Availability Heuristic

We heavily weigh decisions and opinions towards information that is easier to recall

We too easily assume that our memories are representative and true, discounting events that are not immediately recalled when evaluating a decision or belief.

As the long, dark and cold days of winter start to roll in, public health organisations start promoting flu vaccinations to vulnerable segments of the population. My grandparents fit into this group.

Each year they staunchly ignore the advice, explaining, "Do you know they inject you with the flu! Last year, three of our friends developed a really bad case of the flu after being vaccinated".

While hard to quantify, different reports show the vaccine reduces the risk of contracting flu by about 50% to 60%. In the case of my grandparents, that means it is very likely that six out of every ten of their friends who had the flu jab had a much lower risk of contracting it.

However, my grandparents in their eighties are unlikely to recall such specific probabilities. It's much easier to remember friends from their weekly Bingo session who were struck down with the flu in previous years.

And therein lies the problem. Immediate examples that come to our minds when evaluating a specific topic, concept, method or decision weigh much more heavily. The availability heuristic operates on the notion that if something can be recalled, it must be important, or at least more important than alternatives not as readily recalled.

School Shootings

In America, school shootings are considered a relatively new, and devastating phenomenon. The 1999 Columbine High School massacre saw two senior students murder twelve of their fellow students and one of their teachers. It was an event that fundamentally changed the way schools are operated in the United States.

After the shootings, there were a number of high-profile studies and documentaries that examined how school shootings had become an "epidemic" across America. The truth, however, was that there hadn't been an increase in school shootings. Quite the opposite.

During the time when Columbine got major media attention, violence in schools was down by over 30%. Kids were more likely to get shot in school before Columbine, but the media during that time didn't give the public many examples. A typical student, at the time, was three times more likely to get hit by lightning than to be shot by a classmate, yet schools started to guard against shooting as if one could happen at any second.

Like with my grandparents, parents were more easily able to recall fatal school shootings shown in the media than the millions of school children who go to school safely each day. As a result, parents placed pressure on schools to implement protective measures for their children.

As is now clear, recalling an event and estimating the real probability of an event happening are two different things. The availability heuristic distorts our attitudes towards the future.

Word Count

In one of the early studies that pinpointed the availability heuristic, 152 participants were asked to estimate the relative frequency various letters of the English alphabet appeared in the first and third positions in English words from a range of texts (Tversky & Kahneman, 1973). A typical problem read as follows:

Consider the letter K. Is K more likely to appear in:

    1) the first position of a word? Or;
    2) the third position of a word.

Word Count (Tversky & Kahneman, 1973)

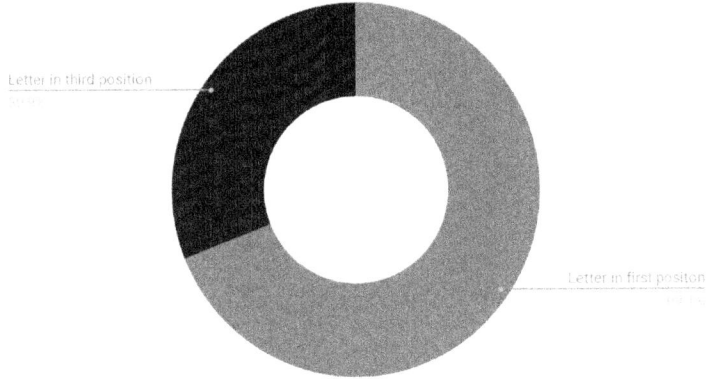

Letter in third position

Letter in first position

Among the 152 participants, 105 (69.1%) judged the first position to be more likely for the letters to appear. Only 47 (30.9%) participants judged the letters to be found more often in the third position of a word. In fact, all the letters used in the study were more commonly found in the third position. Almost 70% of the participants were wrong!

But why? Researchers believed it was easier to recall a word using its first letter (e.g., "K", kangaroo, kitchen, kale), but much harder to think of words where the letter was in the third position ("K"; acknowledge, ask). This is not surprising given we commonly use the first letter of a word to sort alphabetically. It's very rare we need to consciously recall the third letter in a word.

The ease of recall can substantially and unconsciously influence our judgment.

Famous Names (part 1)

Investigating the availability heuristic further, researchers hypothesised the number of examples that could be recalled from memory had the biggest influence on decision-making behaviour. To explore this idea, they set up an experiment in which 185 participants were split into two groups (Tversky & Kahneman, 1973).

One group listened to a researcher who read out one list of names containing nineteen very famous women (e.g., Elizabeth Taylor) and another containing twenty less famous men (e.g., William Fulbright). Similarly, the second group listened to similar lists; however, the genders were reversed. The first contained nineteen very famous men (e.g., Richard Nixon) and the second contained twenty less famous women (e.g., Lana Turner).

Participants were asked to recall as many names as possible from each list they had heard.

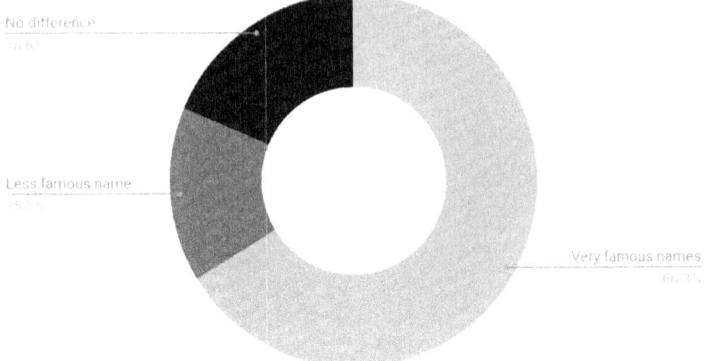

Famous Names (part 1) (Tversky & Kahneman, 1973)

No difference

Less famous name

Very famous names

As expected, 66.3% recalled more very famous than less famous names, only 15.1% recalled fewer very famous than less famous names, and 18.6% participants recalled the same number of very and less famous names. Remember, the smaller list of nineteen names always contained the very famous ones.

Participants remembered more names from the smaller lists of very famous names because they could be brought to mind more easily.

Famous Names (part 2)

You probably think that it's easier to remember famous names. Yes, but herein lies the key part of the experiment. Following the name recall, task participants were also asked to recall which of the two lists they believed contained more names (Tversky & Kahneman, 1973).

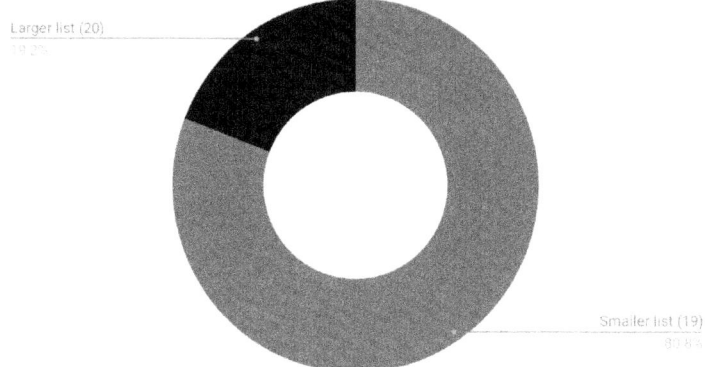

Famous Names (part 2) (Tversky & Kahneman, 1973)

Larger list (20)
19.2%

Smaller list (19)
80.8%

In the results, 80.8% of participants incorrectly judged that the smaller lists of nineteen very famous names had contained more names. Only 19.2% of participants correctly judged which of the two lists was larger! The fact that participants had remembered more very famous names caused them to believe that the list they came from must be longer.

The results suggest that **we judge the frequency of something by the ease with which the relevant examples come to mind. Examples readily recalled, like very famous names, will be judged more numerous than examples less remembered**. The idea is similar to school shootings; we think they are more common because we remember more of them than the alternatives.

Behaviour Traits

Another set of researchers wanted to test the ease of recall explanation more deeply. They believed the ease with which examples come to mind, not the total number of examples that are held in memory, have a greater influence on our decisions and opinions.

In one experiment, forty participants were split into two groups (Schwartz et al., 1991). In one group, half of the participants were asked to recall six examples of their assertive behaviours (e.g., stood up for their own rights). The other group was asked to recall six examples of their unassertive behaviours (e.g., afraid to speak up).

The two groups were then split in half again, with one group of participants in each behaviour condition asked to recall six additional examples of either their assertive or unassertive behaviours, that is, they were asked to recall twelve examples in total.

After writing down the behaviours, participants were asked to recall how difficult they found the task. They were also asked some general questions designed to explore how assertive they felt after recalling them. Participants were asked to answer on a 10-point scale from 1 (relaxed) to 10 (assertive).

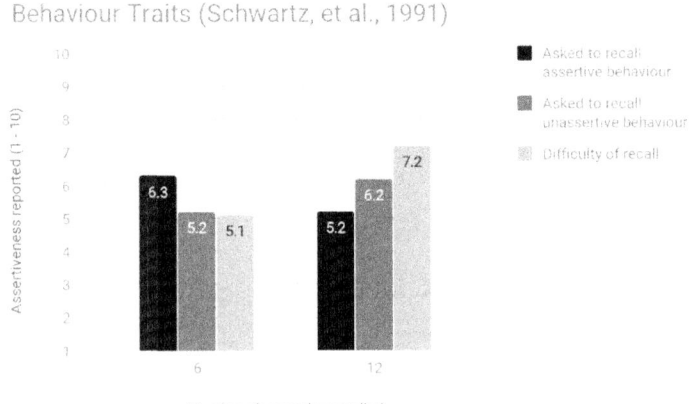

Behaviour Traits (Schwartz, et al., 1991)

Importantly, participants reported that they found it easier to recall six behaviours (M = 5.1) than twelve behaviours (M = 7.2). This was expected. Try it yourself. You can probably remember six of your worst failures or best successes very quickly. After ten it will likely get harder.

Looking at the results of how participants rated their assertiveness, researchers found that participants rated themselves as more assertive after describing six examples of assertive behaviours (M = 6.3) compared with the six unassertive behaviours condition (M = 5.2). Nothing surprising there. However, participants rated themselves as less assertive (M = 5.2) after describing twelve examples of assertive behaviours compared with twelve examples unassertive behaviours (M = 6.2)!

Participants tended to rate themselves as more assertive when they listed fewer assertive behaviours, an exercise they reported easier to complete. Those who listed more assertive behaviours, a task they found challenging, subsequently rated themselves less assertive than the other group asked to recall a smaller number of unassertive behaviours!

Content we can recall more easily heavily influences our decision making (and we typically find it easier to recall things in smaller frequencies, or lists).

Final Exams

Looking at one final experiment, a third set of researchers looked at the effect of uncertainty on the availability heuristic. In line with the motivating-uncertainty effect, which is covered later in this book, researchers believed uncertainty would cause the availability heuristic to become pronounced.

In the experiment, 176 participants were asked to list either three or eight different study methods they could use in order to get an A on their final exams (Vaugh, 1999). Approximately half of the participants were asked for their study methods during the third week of classes, and the other half were asked on last day of classes.

Next, participants were asked to rate how likely they would be to get an A in their easiest and hardest exams on a 9-point scale from 1 (low) to 9 (high). Finally, the participants were also asked to rate the difficulty they experienced in recalling the study methods they had previously listed using the same 9-point scale.

As in the previous experiment, participants found it harder to recall the longer list of study methods. Those asked to list eight study methods reported it to be harder a harder task (M = 5.15) compared to the group asked to recall just 3 (M = 3.45).

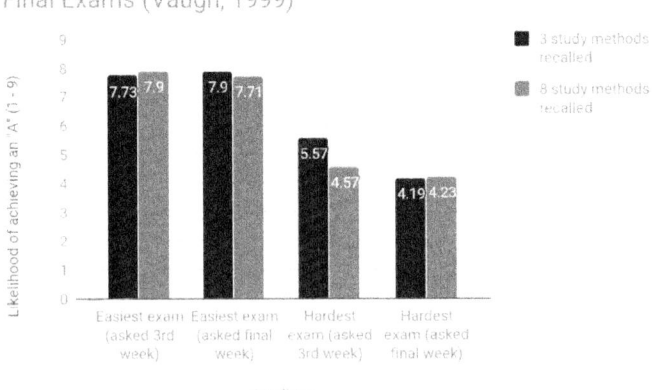

Final Exams (Vaugh, 1999)

As expected, researchers found participants did not use the availability heuristic to predict their grade at the end of the semester. The participants were likely to report a similar likelihood of getting an A, regardless of the number of study methods recalled, on their easiest exam (M = 7.90 for three study methods, M = 7.71 for eight study methods) and their hardest exam (M = 4.19 for three study methods, M = 4.23 for eight study methods). This was because of their certainty in how they would perform in each exam; given it was days away, they did not need to recall any study methods used to make a decision.

Similarly, the participants did not use the availability heuristic to predict their grade on the easiest exam during the third week of the semester. The participants were likely to report a similar likelihood of getting an A, regardless of the number of study methods recalled (M = 7.73 for three study methods, M = 7.90 for eight study methods). Again, researchers believed participants were more certain about the grade they would earn on their easiest exam, perhaps because they did not need to study for it at all, and therefore the study methods did not matter.

Where the outcome was uncertain, that is, for participants estimating their chance of getting an A while only three weeks into the semester, the availability heuristic was clearly observed. Participants who listed and recalled fewer study methods believed they had a much higher likelihood of getting an A (M = 5.57) compared to those who listed and recalled study methods from a larger list (M = 4.57).

The participants who listed fewer study methods were more easily able to recall them and as such believed they had a better chance at the exam. As they could recall more study methods, they were confident in their preparation for success in the coming weeks before the exam.

Pieces of information that come to mind easily are used much more heavily when making a decision when outcomes are uncertain.

Product Gems

1. **Choose where to stand out**
   Make things you want a person to use for decision making (perhaps at a later date) vivid and very easy to bring to mind. For example, this could be achieved with the use of repetition and visual language. Make those things that you do not want them to remember vague, abstract, complex or uncomfortable.

2. **Get people to make assumptions**
   If you want to impress people, have them make assumptions based on your brand or products credibility, success, and ability to suit their needs. Perhaps place your past successes front and centre of any material you produce. For example, list any awards you've won on the homepage of your website.

3. **Be careful when making decisions**
   When making important decisions, pause and think why you are deciding as you are. Is it because of information you have recently received? Who from? Why did they give it to you? Conduct wider research before coming to a conclusion.

4. **Location is important**
   Consumers learn the location of a product and organise their mind accordingly. While you may not remember the name of all three supermarkets on the same corner, your mind remembers that the corner is where to go to find groceries. This idea holds true for all aspects of product marketing. In order to maximise leads, find places that consumers associate with your product's market, such as industry leaders, magazines, trade shows, etc.

5. **Take advantage of free media**

   Try and react quickly to public events or discussions that relate to your product, brand or market. In 2017, there were a number of high-profile cyber-attacks around the world. Many cyber-security software companies successfully used this information to nurture new leads because the events were on every security professional's mind; as a result, these professionals probably judged the likelihood of such an attack happening to them as being far greater following the news.

6. **Keep messaging relevant**

   Too much information can lead to choice paralysis (see: choice paradox). As the availability heuristic demonstrates, it can also make it harder to recall. People might find it difficult to remember your messaging over that of your competitors if it is particularly verbose.

7. **Think about product evaluations**

   In another study, participants were asked to write two recommended improvements to a class (a relatively easy task) and then write two positives about the class. The second group was asked to write ten suggestions for improvements (a relatively difficult task) and then write two positive comments about the class. At the end of the evaluation, both groups were asked to rate the course on a scale from one to seven. The results showed that students asked to write ten suggestions (difficult task) rated the course less harshly because it was more difficult for them to recall the information. Students asked to do the easier evaluation with only two complaints had less difficulty in terms of availability of information, so they rated the course more harshly. Think about the questions you ask for any product evaluations and whether the availability heuristic might be swaying a customer's memory (and potential referrals!) (see: choice-supportive bias).

9. Anchoring Bias

We tend to rely too heavily on the first piece of information seen

During decision making, anchoring occurs when individuals use an initial piece of information to make subsequent judgments. Once an anchor is set, other judgements are made by adjusting away from that anchor, and there is a bias toward interpreting other information around the anchor.

Shopping for new clothes is low on my list of things to spend time doing on a weekend. Unfortunately, due to a strangely shaped pair of feet, I prefer visiting a store in-person to ensure the pair I choose provides a good fit rather than buy through the convenience of an e-commerce store.

A single visit can take upward of an hour trying on the shop's entire inventory in search of the perfect shoe. Take one recent Saturday; after some time tying and untying laces, I found a pair of shoes that were perfect.

I then looked at the price tag. £200! As I start to put them back into the shoebox, the salesperson asks me if I like them. "I do, but £200 is way too much for me," I replied. "No, that pair is currently on sale for £100," the salesman quickly added. "Do you want them now?" £100 was still above my intended budget for new shoes, but a 50% discount seemed huge at the time, so I quickly pulled out my card.

The anchor, the regular price of the shoes, stuck right at the front of my mind and it was impossible to forget it. Comparing the sale price to the original amount had caused me to make an irrational decision: spending way above my budget.

You depend on anchoring every day to predict the outcome of events, to estimate how much time something will take, or how much money something will cost. When you need to choose between options or estimate a value, you need footing to stand on. How much should you be paying for cable? What is a good price for rent in this neighbourhood? You need an anchor from which to compare, and when someone is trying to sell you something, they are more than happy to provide one. The problem is, even when you know this, you can't ignore it.

Anchors can make big numbers seem small, throw estimates out of whack, and lead you into decisions which, in the long view, can seem silly.

New Car Sale

Very few buyers expect to pay the full advertised price for a new car. Walking into the showroom, you're confident of negotiating a good deal, remembering that one time you haggled for some souvenirs in a bazaar on holiday.

You see the price sticker in the car window. Of course, you're not going to pay that. "Who pays the full sticker price?" you wonder. In advance, you decide a strategy of low-balling the salesperson, that is to suggest a seemingly unreasonable first offer for the car. Perhaps you try for 30% lower than the sticker price. Maybe 40% if you're feeling brave. In either case, your bid is still anchored to the sticker price.

As negotiations drag on and knowing you're set on buying the car, you and the salesperson agree on a price that's 15% lower than the advertised value (and they'll throw in an air-freshener too). You later tell friends of the skill involved to obtain such a good deal and offer them some future advice on negotiating.

What you might not know is the sale was also a good deal for the salesperson, and the showroom, and the manufacturer, who all made money off selling you the car. Smart salespeople, and their companies will purposely set the advertised price of a car to allow for a reasonable profit after any negotiations, all while still satisfying the customer who believes they've walked away from a good deal.

The advertised price, the anchor, sets the standard for any negotiations. The buyer's focus will be fixed on the anchor during negotiations to baseline how well they are doing. As a result, they won't stray too far

from it. Even if they use the low-ball technique described above, they can be quickly rebuffed by the salesperson using the anchor to point out how absurd they're being. Prices lower than the anchor can seem more reasonable.

African Countries

Anchoring works in all kinds of situations. It is unavoidable. In one of the first experiments exploring the anchoring bias, researchers asked participants to estimate how many African countries were part of the United Nations (Tversky & Kahneman, 1974). Before they answered, they were first asked to spin a wheel painted with numbers from zero to one hundred, similar to The Wheel of Fortune. However, unlike The Wheel of Fortune, the arrow in this experiment was always rigged to land on either ten or sixty-five.

When the arrow stopped spinning, researchers asked each participant in the experiment to say if they believed the percentage of countries was higher or lower than the number on the wheel. Next, they asked participants to estimate what they thought was the actual percentage of African countries in the United Nations.

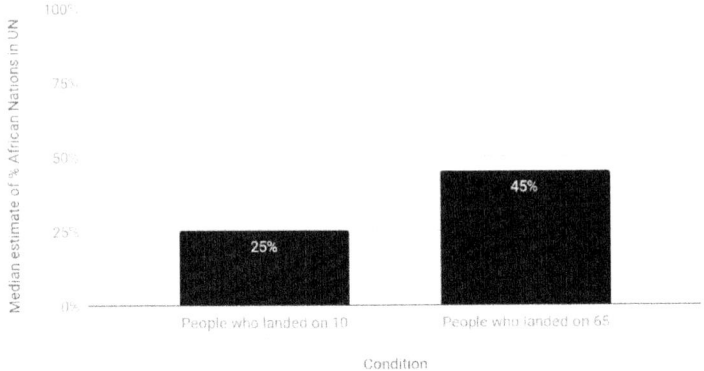

African Countries (Tversky & Kahneman, 1974)

Those who landed on ten in the first half of the experiment guessed around 25% of African countries formed part of the U.N. Those who landed on sixty-five said around 45%. The participants had been locked in place by the anchor set after spinning the wheel.

It is important to note that the participants taking part in the experiment, all living in America, probably had some idea of Africa before the experiment—its size or names of countries—but were unlikely to know the exact number of countries that were in the U.N. They needed to estimate in order to answer the question. To help them do this, they adjusted against the anchor, even though it had no relevance to the question at hand.

When the participants were estimating the number of countries, they were pulling away from the anchor.

Social Security Auction

The anchoring bias can also slip in unannounced in many situations. In 2005, researchers conducted an experiment where a group of MBA students at MIT bid on items in a rather bizarre auction (Ariely et al., 2005).

The researchers held up a bottle of wine, a textbook, a cordless trackball, a cordless keyboard and Belgian Chocolates, describing each item in detail. Each participant was then asked to write down the last two digits of their social security number as if it was the price of the item. For example, if the last two digits were 11, then they should write $11 next to the items. They did this for all items.

Students were then asked if they were willing to pay the price they had written for each item, and the maximum amount they were willing to pay for each of the products (their bids).

Social Security Auction (Ariely et al., 2005)

Product	Range of last two digits of SS number				
	00-19	20-39	40-59	60-79	80-99
Cordless trackball	$8.64	$11.82	$13.45	$21.18	$26.18
Cordless keyboard	$16.09	$26.82	$29.27	$34.55	$55.64
Design book	$12.82	$16.18	$15.82	$19.27	$30.00
Belgian chocolates	$9.55	$10.64	$12.45	$13.27	$20.64
Bottle of wine (Cotes du Rhine)	$8.64	$14.45	$12.55	$15.45	$27.91
Bottle of wine (Hermitage)	$11.73	$22.45	$18.09	$24.55	$37.55

When the researchers analysed the data, they found students with high social security numbers paid up to 346% more than those with low numbers. Participants with social security numbers ending 80 to 99 placed an average maximum bid of $26 for the trackball, while those with numbers ending 00 to 19 were willing to pay, on average, just $9! Writing up the experiment, the researchers noted:

"Social security numbers were the anchor in this experiment only because we requested them. We could have just as well asked for the current temperature or the manufacturer's suggested retail price. Any question, in fact, would have created the anchor."

Mahatma Gandhi

In another experiment exploring the anchoring bias, researchers wanted to test farfetched anchors to test the biases limits. They gathered two groups of students and asked them each a different question about Mahatma Gandhi, the well-known Indian civil rights activist (Mussweiler & Strack, 1997).

The first group were asked whether he died before or after age nine, the second was asked if he died before or after age 140. All participants were then asked to write down how old they thought Gandhi was when he died.

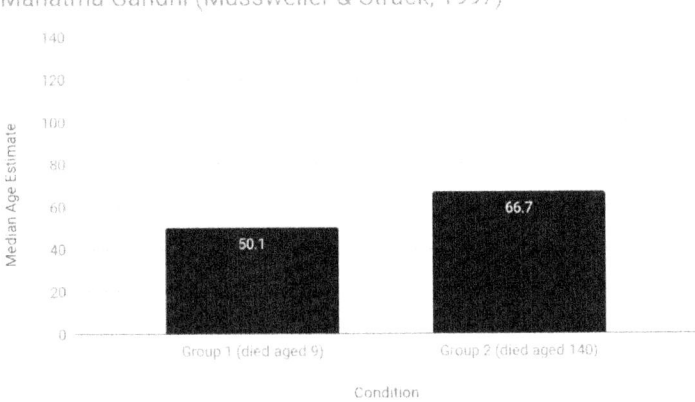

Mahatma Gandhi (Mussweiler & Strack, 1997)

As expected, the first group that were asked the question primed with the low anchor (died before or after age nine) guessed a median age of 50.1 years, 17 years younger than the second group who were primed with the higher anchor and guessed the age of death to be 66.7 years (died before or after age 140).

As in the previous experiment, most participants were unlikely to have known the exact answer to this question. Gandhi was eighty when he died. However, they probably did know a little about Gandhi, and that it was unlikely either of the anchors were correct. Rationally, each group should have disregarded the anchor entirely.

Even when an anchor was clearly incorrect, the students still used it to adjust against because of a lack of other information available.

Mental Arithmetic

The anchoring bias clearly works when a starting point is given, as the previous experiments show. Tversky and Kahneman wanted to further test the anchoring bias based on our ability to compute information.

They gathered two groups of high school students and asked them to each answer a maths question within five seconds (Tversky & Kahneman, 1974).

Group 1 question: 8 x 7 x 6 x 5 x 4 x 3 x 2 x 1
Group 2 question: 1 x 2 x 3 x 4 x 5 x 6 x 7 x 8

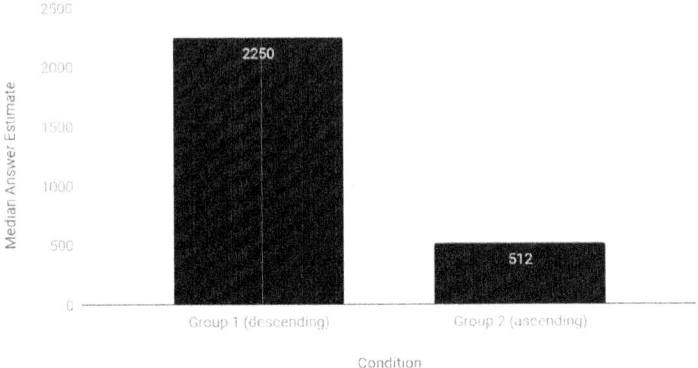

Mental Arithmetic (Tversky & Kahneman, 1974)

The eagle-eyed readers will notice the answers to both questions are the same (the order of numbers is simply reversed). The correct answer to both questions is 40,320. Remember each group only saw one question.

With only five seconds to answer, most students could only compute the sum of the first few digits of the question (English speaking, reading left-to-right). Using this result, they then tried to estimate the answer to the whole question by adjusting away from their calculated sum. This resulted in Group 1, where the numbers were in descending order estimating the answer to be much higher (M = 2250) than Group 2 where the numbers were placed ascendingly (M = 512).

To rapidly answer such questions, we often try to perform a few steps of computation and estimate the answer based on extrapolation and adjustment.

Door-in-the-Face Technique

The foot-in-the-door technique is a persuasion technique discussed earlier in this book. The reversed approach, that is making a deliberately outlandish opening request so that subsequent, milder requests will be accepted, is known as the door-in-the-face technique and is a variation of the anchoring bias.

An experiment that first coined the name of this technique asked seventy-two university students if they would volunteer (unpaid) to chaperone children at a juvenile detention centre (Cialdini et al., 1975).

The participants were split into two groups. One group was first asked to give up two hours each week over a minimum of two years (extreme request). Those that disagreed were then asked if they would chaperone the children for only two hours during a trip to a zoo (small request). The other half of the participants were only asked the small request, to give up two hours to chaperone the children on a trip to the zoo.

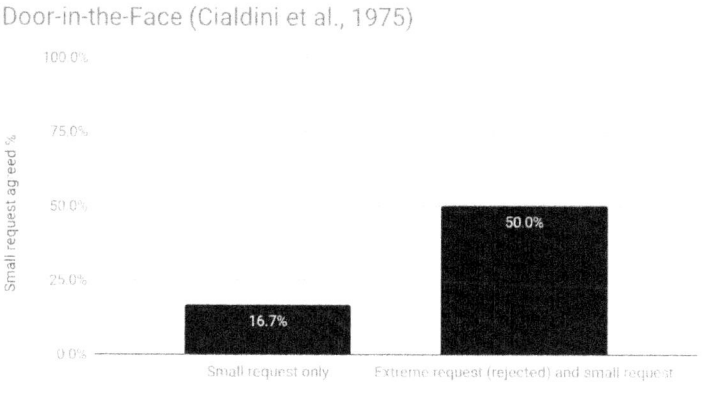

Door-in-the-Face (Cialdini et al., 1975)

Of the participants only asked to volunteer for the small request, just 16.7% of them agreed to give up their time. Astoundingly, 50% of the participants who first turned down the extreme request for two years of their time subsequently agreed to the small request!

It appears that the act of rejecting the first offer, the anchor, was more likely to cause the participant to agree with the other, smaller offer, because the effort of the task was reframed.

Researchers have also hypothesised that this technique works due to the principle of reciprocity. Saying "no" to a large request may make someone feel that they owe a favour to the person who made the request.

Product Gems

1. **Consider pricing tiers**
   Setting a high price for one item makes all others seem cheaper, though only when the price shown is actually plausible (and not some silly amount!). Consider offering tiered pricing. For example, a basic version of a product could be used to form an anchor for a premium product.

2. **Keep anchors realistic**
   Don't set your anchor price too high, or the natural inclination to anchor other choices against this product will greatly diminish. Keep it realistic and relatively in the realm of what else you're selling.

3. **Not everything is an anchor**
   We see the manufacturer's suggested retail price for cars, lawn mowers, and coffeemakers. We get the real estate agent's spiel on local housing prices. But price tags by themselves are not necessarily anchors. They become anchors when we contemplate buying a product or service at that particular price.

4. **Review your product range**
   Think carefully about how you structure your product range and prices. People will anchor whether you intend for them to do so, or not.

5. **Be aware of your target audience**
   Anchoring effects are weaker for individuals with higher cognitive ability (Bergman et al., 2010) and those with experience buying the product you're selling (Alevy et al., 2011). Those selling highly specialised products should take note.

6. **Know the past affects the future**
   Although anchoring works to a lesser effect with those who have already bought the product you're

selling, think about the effect anchoring will have on future sales opportunities. For example, if the renewal cost is much higher than the original price paid, the customer might feel as though they're getting a bad deal (see: inaction inertia effect).

7. **You are not a single source of truth**
In academic research, participants have limited information to work from, but in the real world, a customer can often quickly look something up on their phone. If you're selling a generic product beware of becoming the anchor for your competitors, and vice-versa.

8. **Foster behavioural change**
Giving consumers a preferred value to work from can help influence their behaviour and how they use your product or service. The diet industry uses this concept heavily. Dieters are often told that their daily calorie intake should be 2000 kcal. With the anchor primed their mind, dieters try and maintain their caloric intake based on this figure.

10. Picture Superiority Effect

We can recall pictures much more easily than written words

Concepts that are learned by viewing pictures are more easily and frequently recalled than are concepts that are learned by reading their written word form counterparts.

I've covered IKEA a number of times in my writing, including a whole chapter bearing the retailers name (see: IKEA effect). It is a fascinating store, not least for its effect on time. During one of my many visits, I walked in at lunch-time, astonished to walk out in darkness as dinner time approached.

Whether or not IKEA is a Tardis is a topic of discussion for another book, though one thing is for sure; the winding path that navigates past *every-single-item* for sale must be longer than one kilometre. IKEA "pro's" will well aware of the shortcut to navigate more directly when you know exactly what you need, and don't want to be tempted by additional items.

As I found out on my most recent visit, the friendly employees standing at the entrance can provide you with a store map. I wish they did the same for supermarkets. The map lays out visually how to manoeuvre to the store most effectively based on what you're looking for.

When you finally make it home, many hours later, and start the endeavour of building your purchase the enclosed instructions will prove invaluable. The smiling, illustrated character found in the booklet will show you where each screw, washer and bolt belongs alongside one-line annotations that describe the assembly instructions.

In both these examples, IKEA is making use of the picture superiority effect to support their customers. Visually representing singing picture and textual information helps improve the consumers understanding, and ultimately their satisfaction,

The picture superiority effect is commonly used in instructional design, advertising, technical writing, and other design contexts that require an easy and accurate recall of information.

Infographics

It is said that a picture is worth a thousand words, something advertisers have known this for deceased. Whether it's been a simple application like the Yellow Pages (ads with pictures got more business) or giant billboards in New York's Times Square.

Humans are visual learners: 90% of information transmitted to our brains is visual. Infographics are great examples of turning complex textual data into captivating, memorable imagery but most importantly, make it easier to assimilate.

Asking someone to read a data report requires a lot of attention and time. Turning that report into an infographic streamlines the process while increasing the probability that your reader will retain the information.

Infographics work so well because using text and images together helps people to retain the information. Remember, if it's just words, people will remember less of the information they read. But, if you combine the text with a relevant image, they are much more likely to remember the information! While others may choose to work harder by crafting a perfectly written article or advertisement, it would be a smarter choice to use text and relevant images together.

Using text and images together helps people to retain the information much better than using text alone.

Brand Names (part 1)

Allan Paivio (1971) explains the picture superiority effect with the theory of "dual coding": when we're presented with an image it generates both a verbal and an image code in our brain. When our brain then wants to retrieve information, it finds it easier to locate the images because they have two records, a verbal one and a visual one.

To examine the power of visual imagery, an early experiment was set up testing how consumers remembered brand names and brand logos (Childers & Houston, 1984).

Researchers split a group of participants into two groups:

1. Verbal condition: Participants were shown a list of 20 fictitious adverts from brand names (e.g., Gateway Fence Company). The advert only contained text presented in a range of colours.
2. Pictorial condition: Participants were shown the same list of 20 fictitious adverts from brand names accompanied by a logo that directly portrayed the brand name (e.g., a silhouette of a fence). As before the adverts were presented in a range of colours.

After viewing their assigned adverts, participants were then asked to recall as many of the brand names as possible.

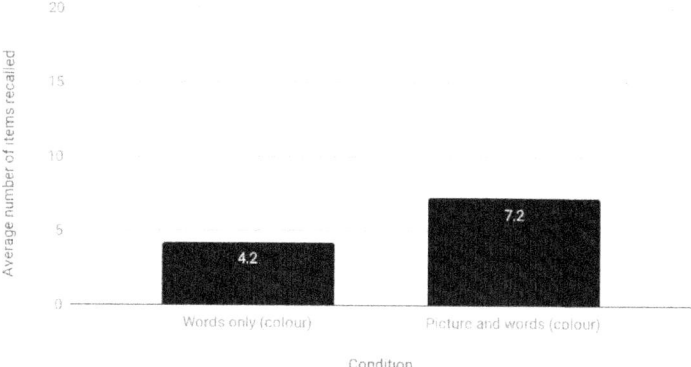

Those participants exposed to adverts in text format remembered far fewer of them (M = 4.3) when compared to those who saw the brand name alongside its logo.

As hypothesised, visual and verbal material was recalled differently. Participants recalled pictures and words together much more than words alone.

Brand Names (part 2)

A number of researchers have also suggested that pictures receive more extensive semantic processing than do words (Intraub & Nicklos, 1985). Semantic processing causes us to relate the word we just heard to other words with similar meanings. For example, giving words meaning or linking them with previous knowledge.

Examining this, the researchers included sensory and semantic variables to the experiment (Childers & Houston, 1984). Before the experiment, all the participants viewed an instruction pamphlet describing the scenario. The participants in both the verbal and pictorial conditions were split into two groups:

1. Sensory processing: participants were presented with adverts that were described with overtly sensory elements, using appearance-related adjectives (e.g., shape, curvature).
2. Semantic processing: participants were presented with adverts described with informational features and semantic adjectives (e.g., strong, good).

As before, after viewing the adverts, participants were then asked to recall as many of the brand names as possible.

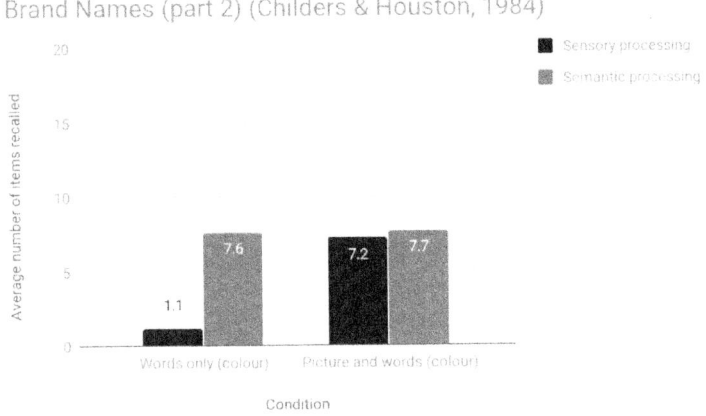

Brand Names (part 2) (Childers & Houston, 1984)

Under immediate recall, pictures far outperformed words under sensory processing (M = 1.1 vs. M = 7.2), while under semantic processing there is only a slight difference (M = 7.6 vs. M = 7.7). Pictorial ads were recalled to a much greater extent than verbal-only ads when encoding focused on the sensory features of stimuli.

It appeared the participants did not code verbal-only sensory messages in their short-term memory leading

to a worse recall. This, in some part, explains why we often have to reread a book before fully understanding the content.

Brand Names (part 3)

The Atkinson–Shiffrin model is a model of memory proposed by Richard Atkinson and Richard Shiffrin (1968). The model asserts that human memory has three separate components:

1. a sensory register, where sensory information enters memory,
2. a short-term store, which receives and holds input from both the sensory register and the long-term store,
3. a long-term store, where information which has been coded in the short-term store is held indefinitely.

The researchers, having previously examined immediate recall (drawing from participants short-term memory stores), then wanted to understand the effect of the picture superiority effect on delayed recall (Childers & Houston, 1984).

Using the same scenario as part 2 of the experiment, this time instead of having participants immediately recall the advert, this time they were asked to return to the lab two days later and recall the adverts.

Brand Names (part 3) (Childers & Houston, 1984)

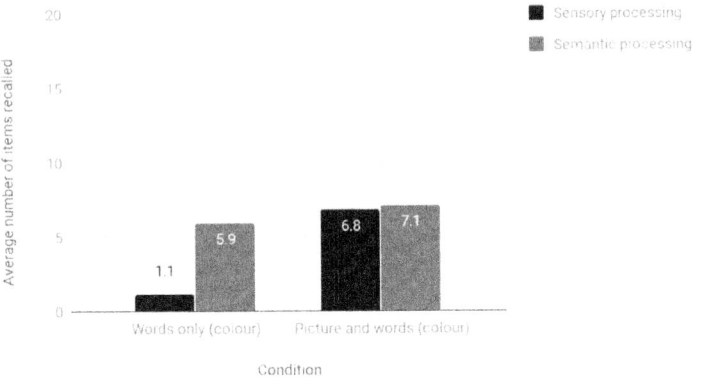

The results from part 3 almost mirror those from part 2 with one notable finding. The participants instructed to examine the adverts semantically recalled the words significantly better two days later having viewed both pictorial and text ads (M = 7.1) compared to text-only ads (M = 5.9). In the previous part of this experiment, there was no significant difference in recall for this group of participants. A picture superiority effect became clearly evident under semantic processing when the recall was delayed.

Visually oriented messages seem particularly appropriate under conditions where audiences are less motivated or capable of semantic processing. Low-involvement consumers and media-paced exposure time (e.g., TV ads) represent these conditions. Visual ads seem to require less frequency of exposure than that necessary for verbal ads to achieve the same effect on long-term memory.

Sugary Drinks

Nudging health-related decisions has been a powerful tool for governments to improve the overall wellbeing of its population (see: present bias). Images have proved a powerful tool in enabling this, as the researcher's second line of analysis uncovered.

A group of Harvard researchers set up a field study in a hospital cafeteria (Donnelly et al., 2018). Over the course of six weeks, researchers tested the impact of product labelling. For consecutive two-week periods, researchers placed one of the following labels on the sugary drinks (more than 12 grams of sugar per bottle) sold in the cafeteria:

1. No warning: There were no changes made to the bottles in addition to the manufacturer's original label.
2. Text warning: The bottles were affixed with a text warning label that read "WARNING: Drinking beverages with added sugar(s) contributes to obesity, diabetes, and tooth decay.
3. Graphic image warning: The graphic warning label included the same text as the text warning label, but also included images portraying obesity, diabetes, and tooth decay that were similarly evocative to those found to be effective on tobacco products.

After the six-week trial, the researchers examined the sales data.

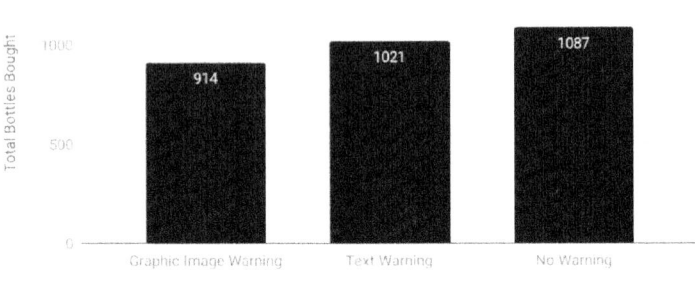

Sugary Drinks (Donnelly et al., 2018)

Of the 3022 sugary drinks sold, during the two weeks where no warning was shown, 1087 drinks were purchased. When the text warning labels were affixed to the bottles, 1021 drinks were sold, and just 914 were sold when graphic image warning labels were placed on the bottles.

At the point-of-sale, graphic image warning labels were much more effective in reducing the number of sugary drinks purchased than text labels. While the text and graphic warning labels conveyed the same facts about health risks, only the more graphic labels were associated with behaviour change.

Evocative images are more likely to quickly capture our attention than text, and in turn, we are more likely to contemplate our actions when presented with them.

Brand Ads

Some experts say we've gone from being exposed to about 500 ads a day back in the 1970s to as many as

5,000 a day today. Online, television, and traditional print adverts are impossible to avoid completely.

Many advertisers hold the assumption that consumers of picture-word messages attend to the pictorial component first. Indirect support for this premise comes from traditional advertising design principles, which advocate the use of pictures in ads for their "attention-getting" ability and the belief that artwork is usually the first part of the advert to be examined (Bolen, 1984).

Aware of the picture superiority effect, a group of researchers wanted to test the effect of images and text on a consumers perception of a brand.

Similar to the previous Brand Name experiment, participants viewed a range of adverts. They were first split into two groups. One was shown adverts with relevant pictures, that is those that pictorially represent the brand name and product class (fence company advert and fence in picture), whereas the other group were shown irrelevant pictures where the images in the adverts bore no relationship to the brand name and may or may not represent the product class.

The adverts were combined with either consistent verbal content (i.e., text that described the same attribute portrayed in the picture) or discrepant verbal material (i.e., text that described an attribute different from the one represented in the picture). Half of each group of participants were exposed to either the consistent or the discrepant text.

Subjects were exposed to each advert for 15 seconds. After viewing all the adverts, they were allowed 10 minutes to write down everything they could remember about the advertisements they had viewed. Researchers developed a total recall score measure that scored each participants recall based on the correct mention of the product category, brand name and specific information, such as phone numbers or locations in the advert.

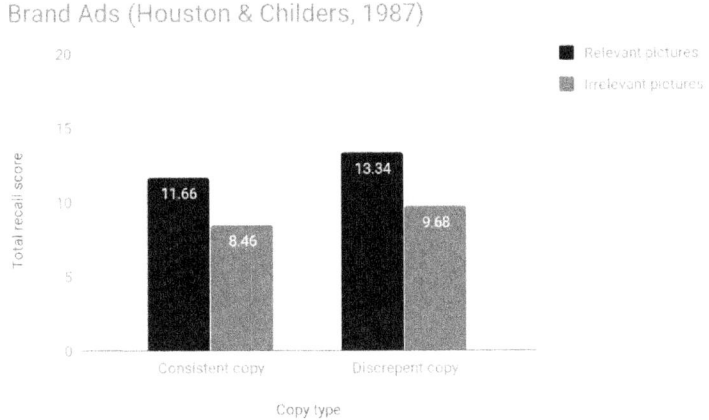

Brand Ads (Houston & Childers, 1987)

Clearly, the relevance of the logo or image to the brand is important in the recall of the advertisement. Those who viewed the relevant images had a superior recall (M = 11.6 for consistent and M = 13.34 for discrepant text) when compared with those participants that were shown the irrelevant pictures (M = 8.46 and M = 9.68).

Most interestingly, the researchers discovered that when the text did not convey the same message as the advert recall was significantly higher (M = 11.6 for irrelevant pictures and M = 9.68 for irrelevant pictures) than when the text was consistent (M = 11.66 and M = 8.46). contradictory to a common belief that the pictorial and verbal components of an advertisement should convey the same message (Schultz, 1981), adverts that display text with differing messages from the imagery appear to be better recalled. Researchers concluded this tactic might capture more of the viewers' attention as they spend more time trying to understand inconsistencies in the advertisement.

The results suggest the picture superiority effect is enhanced, especially in advertisements, where the image matches the consumer's expectation. Surprisingly, it appears the picture superiority effect is further heightened when the text of the advert does not match the imagery presented to the viewer.

Product Gems

1. **Consider the best medium for communication**
   While words are sometimes necessary to communicate complex topics, diagrams and graphics can quickly and easily communicate key information. For example, through using an infographic or video in a blog post.

2. **Capture attention quickly and be sticky**
   The effect is particularly important where an intended action is taken at a later date after consuming the information. Consumers viewing an advertisement might not immediately want or need to purchase a product. In such cases, we are better able to recall pictures, and thus brands or products, at a much later date as they've been dual coded in our long-term memory.

3. **Boost brand recognition**
   The picture superiority effect advantage increases further when people are casually exposed to information and the exposure time is limited. For example, an advertisement for a clock repair shop that includes a picture of a clock will be better recalled than the same advertisement without the picture. People not interested in clock repair who see the advertisement with the picture will also be better able to recall the brand if the need for clock repair service arises at a later time. If you're striving for brand recognition make sure your logo clearly represents your business activities (and avoid text logos).

4. **Keep it simple**
   The strength of the picture superiority effect diminishes as the information becomes more complex. For example, people are able to recall

events from a story presented as a silent movie just as well as events from the same story read as text.

5. **Don't get too creative**
   The effect is strongest when the pictures represent common, concrete things versus abstract things, such as a picture of a flag versus a picture depicting the concept of freedom, and when pictures are distinct from one another, such as a mix of objects versus objects of a single type (see: availability heuristic).

6. **Pictures and words should be consistent**
   Use pictures and words together and ensure that they reinforce the same information for optimal effect. Pictures and words that conflict, create interference and dramatically inhibit recall. Consider the inclusion of meaningful pictures in advertising campaigns when possible, especially when the goal is to build company and product brand awareness.

7. **Be aware inconsistency can sometimes work**
   As shown in the final experiment, recall can be increased when it does not match the imagery conveyed. Viewers pay more attention to incorrect looking adverts as they spend more time trying to understand the content, thus leading to an enhanced recall. Though be careful, you want to be remembered for the right reasons -- "shock & awe" tactics can easily backfire (see: Von Restorff effect).

Now, as we've learned, it's probably a good idea to go back and reread this chapter.

11. Scarcity Bias

We place a higher value on things in limited supply

Whenever choice is limited or threatened, the human need to maintain a share of the limited commodity makes us crave it even more. Scarcity increases the value of any product or service. Scarcity drives people to action, making us act quickly for fear of missing out on an opportunity.

If you're a keen gardener, stones that litter the soil can become frustrating to sift out. These pieces of solid mineral material are tossed aside in pursuit of the perfect vegetable garden. Though not all rocks are created equal.

Diamonds are minerals that occur most commonly in a rock called Kimberlite. Before 1870, finding Kimberlite deposits, and thus diamonds, was a very rare occurrence. Often these rare stones would end up in the hands of royalty lining their ostentatious jewellery.

In 1870, the fledgeling diamond industry struck gold. Enormous deposits of diamonds were discovered in Kimberley, South Africa. Diamonds began to flood the market. As more and more diamonds were mined, they became less scarce, and their price dropped as a result. The owners of the South African diamond mines quickly realised they were making their own investments worthless.

The diamond market may have bottomed out were it not for an enterprising individual by the name of Cecil Rhodes. He began buying up mines in order to control the output and keep the price of diamonds high. By 1888, Rhodes controlled the entire South African diamond supply, and in turn, essentially the entire world supply. One of the companies he acquired was eponymously named after its founders, the De Beers brothers.

De Beers, who are still the world's largest diamond company, now keep tight control of the supply that enters the market. Creating the illusion of scarcity to customers, for what is a fairly abundant resource, has allowed the market to charge a high markup on diamonds.

The perceived scarcity of diamonds is why many of us can justify spending thousands buying them to line engagement rings or other special pieces of jewellery, despite the fact they will lose a significant amount of value once they leave the store.

Even brands that sell a commodity product can use scarcity to attract customers and increase sales.

Black Friday

Black Friday (and now Cyber Monday) are marked clearly in shopping calendars around the world. The event started as an invention of an American organisation, the National Association of Retailers. Their aim; increase retail sales. An aim that has now well surpassed initial expectations.

For those unfamiliar, Black Friday and Cyber Monday events offer a limited number of discounted products to customers. Some retailers see customers queuing for days in advance to grab the best bargains. In many cases, a retail frenzy ensues when the doors finally open.

Scarcity is one of the key factors behind the success of these shopping days. Retailers promote to customers that a limited number of items will be available at a discount. Customers who might not have needed a new TV suddenly attribute additional value to it because of scarcity, turning them into must-have items in conjunction with the discount

Remember, price does not equal value. This is important. Even though these shopping days provide discounts to customers, that is a reduction in price, the value of the product to a customer does not necessarily change. If they don't need a new TV before the event, a discount is not going to change their need for it.

Limited or rare supplies are perceived by people as a threat to their freedom of choice, triggering a reaction to fight the threat and maintain their access to the resource.

Cookie Jar (part 1)

The most famous experiment into scarcity was led by Stephen Worchel, a psychologist at the University of Virginia. In 1975, he recruited 146 participants and asked them to rate the quality of a batch of cookies (Worchel et al., 1975).

Participants were placed in a room with one researcher and one jar of cookies when a second researcher entered the room. Participants were assigned into one of two groups with differing scenarios:

1. Scarce-no change condition: A jar with 2 cookies was placed on the table. The second researcher comes in and asked participants if the supply of cookies was enough.
2. Abundant-no change condition: A jar with 10 cookies was placed on the table. The second researcher comes in and asked participants if the supply of cookies was enough.

Participants were then asked to indicate whether they would like to eat more of the cookie (liking) and how interested in the cookie they were (attraction) based on a 9-point scale from 1 (very much) to 9 (not at all). Each participant was also asked how much the cookie should cost per pound (value).

Cookie Jar (Part 1) (Worchel et al., 1975)

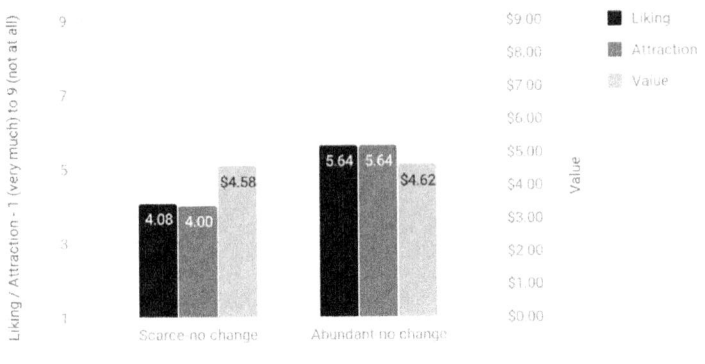

Similar values were reported for each attribute -- liking, attraction, and value -- across both groups. A slightly greater liking and attraction was reported by participants in the scarce condition (M = 4.08 and M = 4.00, respectively) compared to those in the abundant group who saw the 10-cookie jar (M = 5.64 and M = 5.64, respectively). The two groups valued the cookies almost identically.

You might be wondering why the scarcity group did not attribute greater value to the cookies. Remember, these participants were not aware of the 10 cookie, abundant, group. That is, they had no knowledge the available cookies were in much more limited supply.

Marketing and advertising plays a key role in communicating scarcity. Customer must be clearly aware an item is in short supply for the effect to kick in.

Cookie Jar (part 2)

It was clear from part 1 of the experiment that the context of scarcity is important. Scarcity can be natural (i.e., limited natural resource) or introduced artificially (e.g., Black Friday). As an extension of part 1 of the experiment researchers introduced an artificial scarcity (Worchel, 1975):

1. Scarce-change demand condition: A jar with 10 cookies was replaced with a jar of 2 cookies by the second researcher and participants were told this was because the other participants had eaten more of the cookies than expected.
2. Abundant-change demand condition: A jar of 2 cookies was replaced with a jar of 10 cookies by the second researcher and participants were told this was because the other participants had eaten less of the cookies than expected.

As before, all participants were asked to report their liking, attraction, and valuation of the cookies.

Cookie Jar (Part 2) (Worchel, 1975)

When the participants believed the supply of cookies was at risk with other students eating more of them than expected, the participants were willing to pay twice as much (M = $0.72) than those who saw the supply increase due to low demand (M = $0.38).

Similar results are reflected for the reported liking and attraction to the cookies by participants. When the cookies became more scarce liking and attraction was high (M = 2.25 and M = 2.33, respectively) conversely participants in the abundance group reported much worse reviews (M = 7.17 and M = 6.58, respectively).

Participants placed more value and attractiveness on cookies when they knew demand was high and the supply of remaining cookies was limited. As such participants were more willing to act quickly for fear of missing out on the opportunity.

Cookie Jar (part 3)

Though artificial scarcity can be a powerful tool, the reason for scarcity is also important. To test this, the researchers added a third scarce condition to the experiment (Worchel, 1975):

1. Scarce-no change condition: A jar with 2 cookies was on the table. The second researcher came in and asked if the supply of cookies was enough.
2. Scarce-change demand condition: A jar with 10 cookies was replaced with a jar of 2 cookies by the second researcher and participants were told this was because the other participants had eaten more of the cookies than expected.

3. Scarce-change accidental condition: A jar of 10 cookies was replaced with a jar of 2 cookies by the second researcher and participants were told this was because the second researcher had placed the first jar there by accident.

As before, participants were then asked to report their liking, attraction, and valuation of the cookies.

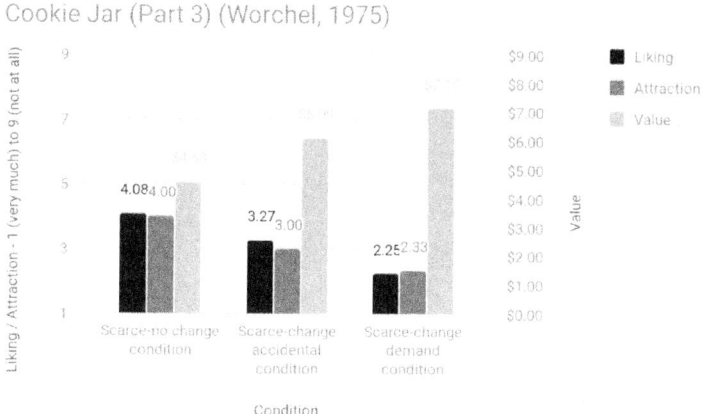

Cookie Jar (Part 3) (Worchel, 1975)

As expected, when the level of scarcity was unknown, participants valued the cookies the least in value (M = $4.58), attraction (M = 4.00), and liking (M = 4.08) across all three conditions.

Interestingly, when scarcity was introduced as a result of other participants consuming more cookies than expected, the participants reported the highest ratings for in value (M = $7.15), attraction (M = 2.33), and liking (M = 2.25) across all three conditions. These ratings were significantly higher than when scarcity was introduced as a result of an accident, and not necessarily as a result of competition with other participants for the cookies, this includes reported ratings for (M = $6.09), attraction (M = 3.00), and liking (M = 3.27) across all three conditions

Demand and scarcity are closely linked. If we feel others are competing for the same scarce resource our interest and valuation of it is greater than a similar resource that is scarce but not in as high demand. Scarcity is a powerful tool to use in conjunction with social proof (see: social default bias).

Cookie Jar (part 4)

In the first three parts to the experiment participants were all made aware there was a number of other participants in the study left to interview. Put another way, researchers introduced estimated future demand to the experiment (Worchel, 1975). If an offer is particularly good, we are likely to believe others will not want to miss out when given a chance increasing our likelihood to act.

To validate this thinking, researchers split the participants further into two groups:

1. High participation: Participants were told there was still a large number of subjects to be run in the study (this was the condition used for the first three parts of the experiment).
2. Low participation: Participants were told that there weren't many participants left to take part in the experiment due to the high costs of the study.

Researchers examined these two groups using the scarce-change demand condition used previously, where a jar with 10 cookies is replaced with a jar of 2 cookies by the second researcher and participants told this was because the other participants had eaten more of the cookies than expected.

Participants were then asked to report liking, attraction, and valuation of the cookies as in the previous parts of the experiment.

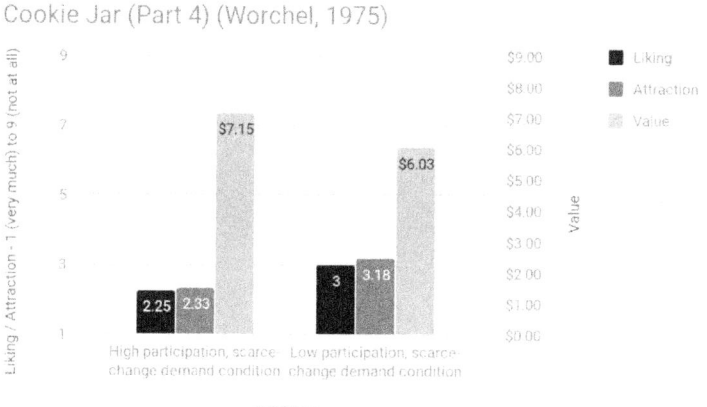

Cookie Jar (Part 4) (Worchel, 1975)

Demand was still in the participant's minds because they knew the cookie supply had been reduced by greedy participants who had gone before them.

However, the low participation group were now acutely aware that there were not many others taking part in the experiment too. Despite having the same number of cookies available and the same freedom to them as the high participation group, those in the low participation group ranked all three measurements lower for value (M = $6.03), attraction (M = 3.18), and liking (M = 3.00) than those in the high participation group.

Participants perceived a false reduction in scarcity. Their thought process being; the fewer people taking part after them, the lower the likelihood of all the

cookies being taken and vice-versa. Put another way; a reduction in future scarcity. The results again highlight the importance of the basic economic theory of demand and supply.

Campbell's Soup

In the modern world, commodity products line our supermarket shelves. We can buy virtual products, like movies or apps, on-demand. Mass-production lines roll thousands, if not millions, of products out to consumers daily. As a result, the concept of artificial scarcity has been adopted by retailers.

At first you might think it is counter-intuitive to limit the number of a product a customer can buy in an attempt to increase sales. One group of researchers set out to test this theory in three real U.S. supermarkets (Wansink, 1998).

Researchers placed displayed at the end of an aisle advertising a variety of Campbell's soups for sale at a discount, $0.79 a can. The regular price was $0.89. Three different signs were used across three consecutive evenings each with different purchase limits for the promotion:

1. No purchase limits
2. Limit of 4 per person
3. Limit of 12 per person

The researchers then counted the number of shoppers who subsequently made a purchase of the soups on offer (906 customers) and how many each customer had purchased in total.

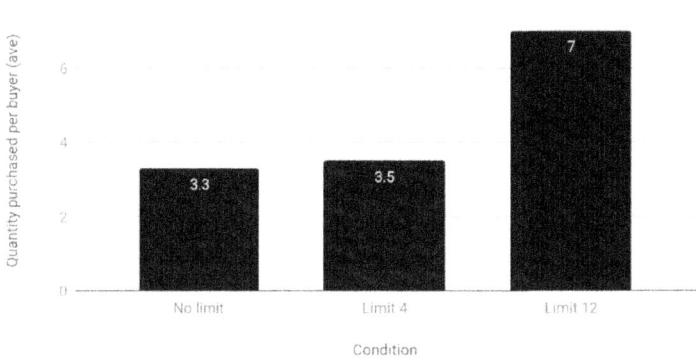

Campbell's Soup Sale (Wansink, 1998)

When items were freely available to purchase at a discount without limitation, buyers of Campbell's soup during the promotion purchased an average of 3.3 cans each. When a limit of four cans was introduced, buyers purchased an average of 3.5. It gets really interesting when considering the promotion when customers were limited to 12 cans each. Buyers purchased an average of 7 cans each -- twice as many the other two conditions despite no change in price.

Scarce promotions are powerful as they harness a consumers' genuine feeling about the brands they are purchasing. Such promotions make the retailer appear neutral by creating an insinuation the offer is so good the store might actually be losing money.

These types of promotions also make use of other cognitive biases, anchoring (see: anchoring bias) and social proof (see: social default bias). The anchor sets an expectation of what other customers are purchasing creating a baseline social norm for the unwitting customer.

Product Gems

1. **Communicate scarcity effectively**
   As demonstrated in the first part of the Cookie Jar experiment, customers need to be clearly aware of scarcity if it exists. For products that are naturally known to be scarce, this is an easier task. However, for commodity type products consider bringing in an element of artificial scarcity.

2. **Publicise short supply due to high demand**
   Customers are competing with each other, in part due to social proof (see: social default bias). Knowing this, limit the supply of goods on offer to create scarcity and in-turn even higher demand. For example, a supermarket might advertise that it is seeing high-demand for cold beers during a particularly hot period to encourage customers to make a purchase during their visit, rather than wait and risk missing out.

3. **Use time-based scarcity**
   If your product does not lend itself well to short-supply based promotions, consider time-based promotions. Announce to customers that if they don't purchase soon, they'll miss out on the opportunity to do so. Many internet-based retailers are good at this. For example, Amazon runs yearly Prime Day events where a certain number of each product is discounted for one day only.

4. **Limit access to your product or service**
   We want what others can't have. The human need to maintain a share of the limited commodity makes us crave it even more. Limiting access to features like information, groups or spaces can prove powerful. Research has shown that censorship made people place a higher value on the restricted

features than those that were not because exclusivity made them feel special (Deng & Pekec, 2013).

5. **Use other biases to enhance the effects**
   Clearly communicate a limit to the number of products a customer can purchase, as demonstrated in the Campbell Soup sale experiment. Anchoring (see: anchoring bias) and social proof (see: social default bias) combined with scarcity will increase the attractiveness of a promotion, and in turn, sales

6. **Experiment with limited edition products**
   Many companies capitalise on the effects of scarcity by offering variations of their most successful products for a "limited time only". A very good example of this is Nestle's Kit Kat. They periodically offer new flavours for a limited time period. The promotions are often so successful a competitive secondary market for sold out editions, namely via eBay, is established creating even greater demand via word-of-mouth.

12. Peak-End Rule

We primarily judge a past experience by its most intense point and how it ended

We judge an experience by its most intense point and its end, as opposed to the total sum or average of every moment of the experience.

One summer, many years ago, I remember vividly watching the Royal Philharmonic Orchestra performing at the Royal Albert Hall. The performance looked to be sold out—there was no sign of an empty seat.

Now, I'm not an expert, but what I saw and heard was impressive, as the open-mouthed concert-goers around me would attest. The conductor was waving his arms around manically, bringing the woodwinds, brass, percussion, and strings sections together beautifully.

At one point, the booming acoustics amplified by the venue died down to a single clarinet. It was a beautiful solo. That was until a new sound rung out—a mobile phone ringing. The music had been ruined. People's expressions of awe turned to frowns for the remaining five minutes of the performance. Thirty minutes of beauty had been destroyed by what happened in a few moments at the conclusion.

We tend not to perceive the overall experience when judging past events but rather how the experience was at its peak (e.g., pleasant or unpleasant) and how it ended. The feeling of the peak and end dictates how we remember our experiences.

Since most consumer interactions have set beginnings and ends, they fit the peak-end rule perfectly. There is a real opportunity to dramatically change your customer's perception and drive the behaviour you want, without changing your fundamental product or service.

AT&T

AT&T, a popular mobile phone provider in the US, noticed that it could take several minutes after a customer entered one of their stores for an associate to be available to help. This caused significant anxiety for customers, who would sometimes wonder if they were next, and how long the wait might be. This led to them reporting dissatisfaction, regardless of how the rest of the in-store experience played out.

After many unsuccessful attempts trying to solve this problem, AT&T's research team found that by quickly greeting a customer, their perception measurably improved the overall experience. They did this by greeting each customer entering a store within ten seconds or ten feet from the door. The AT&T staff would also shake hands with the customer at the end of every interaction, creating a very deliberate, positive moment at the end of the experience.

Not only did the customers greeted in this way report increased satisfaction of the experience, when asked in a survey afterwards, the customers who were greeted quickly also estimated that the waiting time was shorter than it actually was. By changing a simple policy, AT&T turned a negative "peak" into a positive one, which drastically improved customer experience.

Cold Water

In one of the most widely known experiments examining the peak-end rule, thirty-two participants were subjected to two different versions of a single unpleasant experience (Kahneman et al., 1993).

The first trial had participants submerge one of their hands in cold water with a temperature of 14°C (57.2°F) for 60 seconds (short trial). The second part of the experiment had participants submerge their other hand in 14°C water for 60 seconds, but then keep their hand submerged for an additional 30 seconds, during which the temperature was raised slightly to 15°C (59°F) (long trial).

During the trial, participants were asked to record how they were feeling using a dial between 0 (no pain) to 10 (extreme pain). They were also asked to rate overall discomfort following the experiment. Finally, participants were then asked which trial they would choose repeat.

Real-time measures of discomfort were essentially identical for the short trial (M = 8.44) and for the first 60 seconds of the long trial (M = 8.34). Remember, both trials were equally unpleasant for the first 60 seconds as the water temperature was identical. The gradual increase in water temperature during the final 30 seconds of the long trial caused a significant drop in the discomfort reported by participants (M = 6.80).

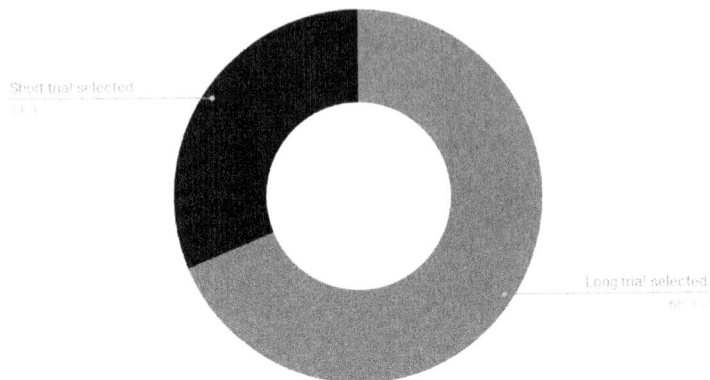

Cold Water (Kahneman et al., 1993)

Short trial selected

Long trial selected

When asked which trial they would repeat, twenty-two of the thirty-two (68.8%) participants were more willing to repeat the longer trial, despite prolonged exposure to uncomfortable temperatures. The participants chose more pain over less pain. Participants also said that the longer trial was less painful overall, less cold, and easier to cope with. Some even reported that it took less time!

It was concluded that participants chose the long trial simply because they remembered the lower discomfort at the end of the experiment, when the temperature increased, and liked this memory better than the alternative (or disliked it less).

The results also suggest our perception of time is affected in recalling experiences of aversive nature.

Colonoscopy (part 1)

Researchers saw similar results when studying patients who had undergone a colonoscopy examination, a routine medical procedure. For this study, people who were scheduled for a colonoscopy agreed to take part in an experiment (Redelmeier & Kahneman, 1996). Given the colonoscopy was being carried out for genuine medical investigation, the actual time of each procedure varied considerably, between 4 and 67 minutes for each colonoscopy. Patients had no knowledge of the procedure length in advance.

In this experiment, participants were split into two groups. Participants in the first group had the colonoscopy conducted as normal (conventional procedure, more painful). For the second group, the researchers wanted to minimise the level of pain during the final minutes of the procedure and thereby allow the patient to retain a more positive memory of the experience. To do so, the tip of the colonoscope was allowed to rest in the rectum for up to three minutes prior to removal (modified procedure, less painful).

During the trial, participants were asked to record how they were feeling using a dial between 0 (no pain) to 10 (extreme pain) every 60 seconds. They were also asked to rate overall discomfort following the experiment.

Upon examining the data, researchers found no significant difference between the two groups in the level of experienced pain during the initial part, the middle part, and the worst part of the colonoscopy procedure. As expected, the level of pain during the final part of the procedure was lower for patients who received the modified procedure instead of the conventional procedure (M = 1.7 vs M = 2.5).

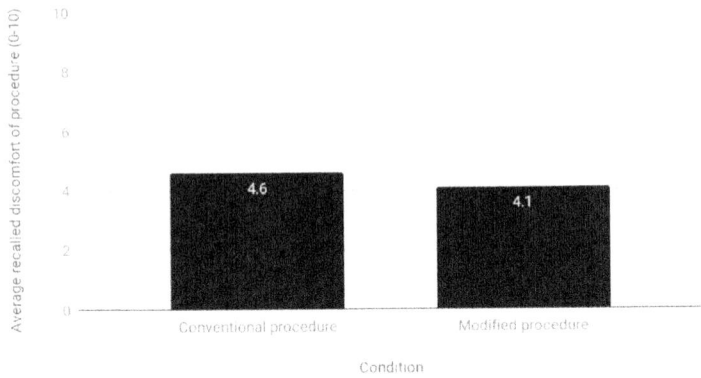

Colonoscopy (part 1) (Redelmeier & Kahneman, 1996)

Curiously, patients who received the modified procedure remembered significantly less total pain (M = 4.1) compared to the conventional procedure (M = 4.6).

Patients memories of painful medical procedures largely reflect the intensity of pain at the worst part and at the final part of the experience, as opposed to the average overall duration of pain.

Colonoscopy (part 2)

Researchers also asked participants, prior to their colonoscopy, whether they had previously undergone the procedure and subsequently monitored them to observe if they returned for a routine follow-up colonoscopy (Redelmeier & Kahneman, 1996).

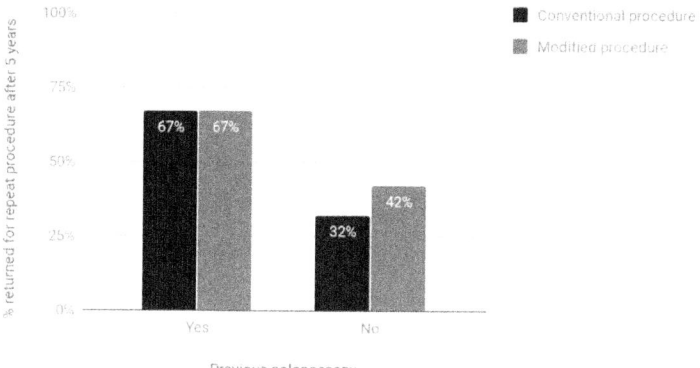

Colonoscopy (part 2) (Redelmeier & Kahneman, 1996)

In the experiment, 42% of the participants who had never received a colonoscopy before and had the modified procedure returned for a repeat procedure. For those the participants that had never received a colonoscopy before and had the conventional procedure, only 32% returned for a repeat procedure. Researchers again concluded this was because a less painful end in the modified procedure led patients to evaluate the procedure, with no prior experience of it, more positively than those who faced the conventional, more painful, procedure.

Those who had undergone a colonoscopy previously had identical rates of return, 67% across both procedures.

Not only do experiences of painful medical procedures largely reflect the intensity of pain at the final part of the experience, but patients' memories of the past may also influence their decisions about the future.

DVDs

Another group of researchers wanted to test if the peak-end rule also affects our experiences when considering material goods, rather than just pain.

In the experiment, 104 participants, part of an existing mailing list, were emailed and informed they had won some DVDs from a raffle they had previously entered (Do et al., 2008).

In the emails, the participants were presented with the opportunity to select free DVDs from two lists. List A consisted of ten movies that were rated highly (very pleasing experience), while List B consisted of ten movies that had an average rating (mildly pleasing experience).

The participants were randomly divided into one of five groups:

1. Group A could select a DVD from List A only
2. Group B could select a DVD from List B only
3. Group C could select a DVD from List A and a second DVD from List B
4. Group D could select a DVD from List B and a second DVD from List A
5. Group E could select a DVD from List A and a second DVD from List A

The participants in groups that were told they had won two DVDs—Groups C, D and E only—were only made aware they could make a second choice after choosing the first DVD.

After making all of their DVD selections, participants were asked to rate how pleased they were with the overall experience of receiving the DVD offer on a scale that ranged from 1 (least pleased) to 7 (most pleased).

DVDs (Do et al., 2008)

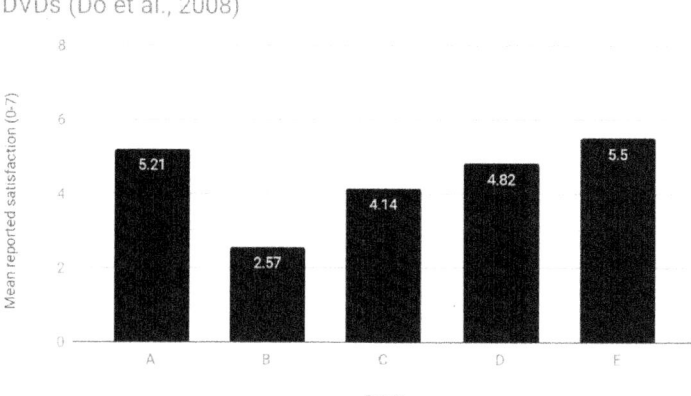

As hypothesised, researchers found that those offered the very pleasing experience, selecting DVDs from list A only (Group A), reported significantly higher levels of satisfaction of the experience (M = 5.21) than the participants selecting DVDs from list B (Group B) only (M = 2.57).

It would appear that bad experiences can be saved. Participants selecting DVDs from list B (Group B) reported far less satisfaction (M = 2.57) than those who selected DVDs from list B and then DVDs from list A (Group D) (M = 4.14). The experience was saved with the addition of a second prize.

The results of this study support the idea that the effects found in retrospective evaluations of pain are also applicable to evaluations of pleasure.

Product Gems

1. **Service recovery is key**
   Negative occurrences in any customer interaction can be counteracted by establishing a firmly positive peak and end. If a mistake is made and immediately corrected, customers tend to forgive easily. This can be achieved in many ways, such as giving out free samples, proactive after-sales care via social media or asking staff members to smile as they hold the shop door for customers as they leave.

2. **Identify some peak positive experiences**
   You know of experiences that customers have appreciated in the past. Use these to create better future experiences when required. For example, a great restaurant owner might serve a complimentary small dessert at the end of a meal, making it seem less expensive! Even during online-based sales, a sincere thank you after purchase can make a real difference to the overall customer experience, and subsequently their likelihood to return and refer.

3. **Look out for peak negative experiences too**
   Experience highlights some frequent customer complaints, too. Addressing these as a priority is a good idea. If you cannot eliminate some known negative experiences systematically, try to right perceived wrongs immediately. This will help with your customer experience.

4. **It's your job to fix mistakes**
   A really great salesperson who helps with an exchange can erase negative experiences along the way. The long wait in line and the bad music in the changing room will be forgotten.

5. **Design empathic product experiences**
   If things go wrong, which they naturally do, whether through the fault of the consumer or a failure of the product experience itself, allow flexibility, humility, and an opportunity to save the relationship.
6. **Don't panic if you make minor mistakes**
   When a small mistake is made, you might be tempted to spend hours fixing it. While this might seem like good practice, think about the opportunity cost of doing so. A simple mistake might be forgotten by a prospect in favour of the peak positive experience.
7. **Apply to meetings and presentations**
   Have you ever heard the phrase "go out on a high"? The peak-end rule proves there is science behind it. For speakers looking to get a point across, make sure it is made at the peak and end of the talk.
8. **Create positive memories for your team**
   Managers should create positive moments for their staff, as well as treat them pleasantly when they leave at the end of each day. This will positively affect their memories of the workday which will, in turn, lead to them staying loyal and motivated.
9. **Communicate carefully**
   As shown in the DVD experiment, the way choices are presented can help them be remembered more favourably if positioned in the right way. Instead of just winning DVDs, the participants won "highly rated" DVDs.

13. Inaction Inertia Effect

Missing an offer makes us less likely to buy in the future

Foregoing a very attractive opportunity decreases our willingness to go for subsequent opportunities.

The concept of a sale is still relatively new in the world of commerce. It was once the case that only a handful of shops would hold sales at the very end of each year to get rid of old and hard to sell stock. Whole families marked days in their diary to pick-up bargains that would see them through the following year.

Other retailers soon realised the benefit of holding sale events and they quickly became more widespread. The increased revenues that resulted from customers buying in bulk rung loudly in the heads of management teams who realised there was an opportunity to make even more money by holding even more sales. Walking around a shopping centre, it would appear that every store, regardless of what they're selling, is running a sale today.

Retailers now vie for business using aggressive discount strategies that include traditional sales but also loyalty rewards and one-off discounts. Many would argue that customers have never been in a better position when it comes to getting a good deal.

Though good deals come at a cost. Those who missed out on purchasing a television for 50% off in a sale by just one day might not be so pleased. What's worse, this disappointment and regret is going to make them think again about buying that television at the normal price. Think back to the last time you saw something on sale. When the object went back to its normal price, did you go out and get it?

The inaction inertia effect would suggest you didn't. Once we see a lower price on a product, our perceptions of its value change. In our heads, we align the perceived value of the product with the lower discounted price. If we didn't move before, we're definitely not going to move in the future if the cost is higher.

Discounting can be highly beneficial, but you should think about the wider "post-sale regret" it can lead to for your customers.

New Camera

When I was a teenager, my father used to return from business trips to America with gifts acquired on his travels. At the time, the exchange rate between the UK Pound and the US Dollar was very favourable. During the early 2000s, there were often cases where electronics were 50% cheaper in America.

One particular year, I really wanted a new camera with a retail price of £200 in the UK. My father knew he could purchase it much more cheaply in the US, exclaiming, "£200 is far too expensive for that camera". As such, he promised to buy it for me on his next trip, six months away.

Crossing each day off my calendar, the day eventually came, and it was well worth the wait. Not only did I get the camera, but my father managed to save 60% compared to purchasing the identical model in the UK.

The significantly discounted price of the camera, thousands of kilometres away, had reframed my father's perceived value of it. In turn, this led him to postpone purchasing it until he could get it for the lower price.

Ski Trip (part 1)

Missed opportunities happen all the time. Sometimes we choose to miss them intentionally, perhaps the opportunity to have dinner with our in-laws. On other occasions, they are missed unintentionally or for reasons beyond our control, due to last-minute work commitments, for example.

In this experiment, 24 participants were split into two groups (Arkes et al., 2002). Half the participants were told that during the previous year they had purchased a ski pass on promotion for $40 (took opportunity). The other half were told they had missed the same promotion for the pass the previous year (missed opportunity).

Both groups were then told to imagine that they were thinking of buying the same ski pass for the upcoming ski season; however, the promotion this year was less favourable with discounted ski passes available for $90, reduced from $100.

All participants were then asked to rate their likelihood of buying the $90 ticket for the upcoming season on a 10-point scale from 1 (not at all likely) to 10 (extremely likely).

Ski Trip (part 1) (Arkes et al., 2002)

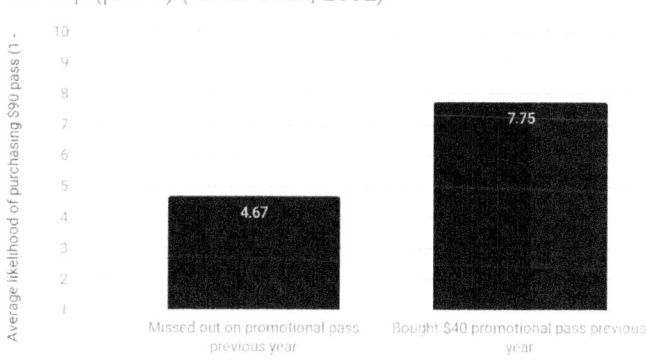

Those who managed to buy the discounted ski pass for $40 the previous season were much more likely to buy it the following year for $90 (M = 7.75) than those who missed out on buying the discounted pass the previous year (M = 4.67).

Researchers believed the regret experienced previously led to an inaction inertia effect; when a previous opportunity to purchase the product was missed, participants were less likely to take advantage of a similar future opportunity.

Ski Trip (part 2)

A saving of $60 on a ski trip could buy a nice meal, or in some more expensive resorts I've been to, about one beer. In the first part of the experiment, the missed discount represented a 60% saving. Researchers were sure the greater regret experienced was directly related to the size of the discount missed and the influence of the inaction inertia effect.

In a follow-up experiment, 135 participants were asked to imagine a similar scenario to that of part 1 (Arkes et al., 2002). In this version, the participants were split into two groups; half the participants were told they had missed the opportunity to purchase a ski pass on promotion for $40 instead of the $100 regular price (large discount missed), while the other half were told they had missed a similar promotion where the pass was priced at $80 instead of $100 (small discount missed). All participants were told that they still had the opportunity to purchase the pass at a slightly discounted price of $90.

Participants were then asked to rate their likelihood of buying the $90 pass on promotion on a 10-point scale from 1 (not at all likely) to 10 (extremely likely). On a similar 10-point scale, participants were also asked to rate the regret they experienced because of missing the promotion from 1 (no regret at all) to 10 (a great deal of regret).

Ski Trip (part 2) (Arkes et al., 2002)

Those who missed out on the larger discount were significantly less likely to purchase the $90 discounted pass (M = 5.98) versus those who had missed the smaller discount when the pass was on offer for $80 (M = 7.71). These participants also reported much greater levels of regret (M = 7.66) than those who missed out on the $80 promotion (M = 4.73).

The cost of missing the discount was closely related to the amount of regret experienced. Those who reported greater levels of regret suffered more from the inaction inertia effect.

Ski Trip (part 3)

Researchers believed the discounts led the participants to re-evaluate the value of the pass. That is, the promotion caused participants to value the pass as less valuable than the normal price because of the discount's influence.

One good example of this is when large discounts are applied. When the product goes back to full price, customers might believe the seller is earning significant profits from selling the product if they were willing to sell previously for a significant discount. Put another way; customers might believe the seller is "ripping them off".

To test this, researchers asked the participants one final question: "what is the highest amount you believe you would now be willing to pay for a ski pass in this situation?" (Arkes et al., 2002).

Ski Trip (part 3) (Arkes et al., 2002)

As expected, those who missed out on the $80 promotion, the small discount condition, were willing to pay over $10 more for the pass (M = $96.97) than those who missed the $40 ski pass promotion, the large discount condition (M = $84.05). Interestingly, participants in the small discount condition were willing to pay almost as much as the regular price of $100 for the ticket, and more than the $90 discount currently on offer to them!

Participants had reframed the perceived value of the ski pass based on the discount they had previously missed out on. Larger discounts significantly lowered

the amount participants were willing to pay in the future.

Couch Sale

In many cases, time reduces our feelings of regret (see: sunk cost fallacy). Researchers assumed time would have the same effect on the inaction inertia effect; while consumers might lower their perceived value of a product immediately after missing a discount, they will eventually rebalance their value estimations towards the original product value over time.

To examine this, an experiment was conducted studying the buying behaviour of sixty-three participants (Putten et al., 2013). Each participant was told to imagine a scenario where they needed to buy a new couch.

The participants were split into three groups. The first group were told a couch they wanted to buy was on sale with a 50% discount in a furniture shop window they had passed the previous day (short miss). The second group was given the same scenario but told they had seen the discounted couch in the furniture shop window two months ago (long miss). Both these groups were told, when they returned on the day of the experiment, that the sale had ended either the day before or two months previously, for the short and long-time difference groups respectively. Both groups were also told that despite missing the 50% sale, the couch was still on sale at a 20% discount. A third group was simply told to imagine this was the first time they visited the store and the couch they wanted to purchase had a 20% discount applied (no miss).

All three groups of participants were then asked to rate their likelihood of buying the couch with the 20% discount applied on a 10-point scale from 1 (not at all likely) to 10 (extremely likely).

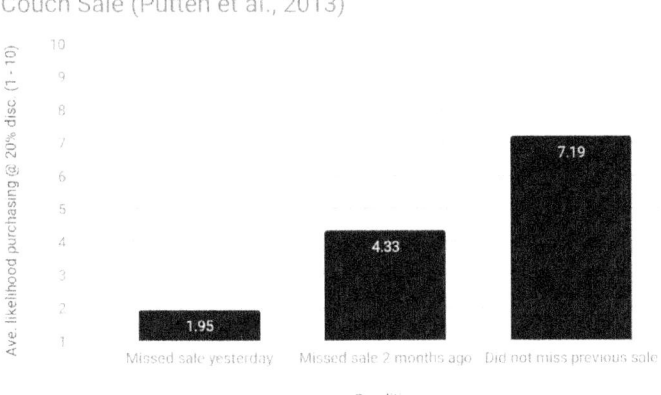

Couch Sale (Putten et al., 2013)

When there was no regret, that is the participants did not know they had missed a sale, their intent to purchase was significantly higher (M = 7.19) than those who missed the sale two months ago (M = 4.33) and those who missed the discount the previous day (M = 1.95).

Initial regret coupled with product devaluation might inhibit customers from buying a product immediately after it has been on sale. However, this counterfactual or 'what-if' thinking reduces over time.

The results suggest that retailers should expect a significant drop in sales for products immediately after a sale ends, with demand slowly increasing again with time.

Rome Trip

The prevalence of retail sales is widespread. Some shops appear to hold sales with regular frequency. For commonly supplied products that are not immediately required, for example, a favourite brand of drink in a supermarket, consumers might forego the opportunity to buy at the regular price opting to wait for a sale they believe is coming up soon or "just around the corner". Researchers examined this using a unique sale and regular sale for a holiday package.

In this experiment, 80 participants were told to imagine that a local travel agency was offering a three-day trip to Rome (Putten et al., 2013). Half of the participants were told the offer was a one-off because the travel agency was celebrating its 25th anniversary (unique sale), the other half were not given any information about the reason for the sale and they were under the impression the discount was part of regular sale held by the travel agency (regular sale).

Next, half of the participants were told they had missed out on booking the trip while it was on sale for €100 instead of the usual €199 (larger difference), the other half were told they had missed booking the trip on sale for €165 (small difference). Both groups of participants were told they could still book the trip for €170.

After learning this, participants were then asked to rate their likelihood of purchasing the trip to Rome for €170 on a 10-point scale from 1 (not at all likely) to 10 (extremely likely).

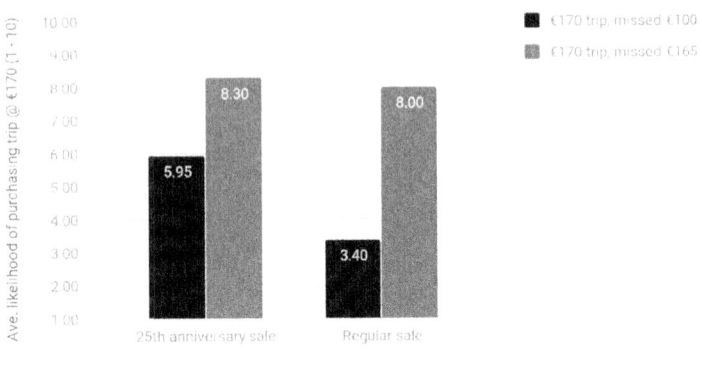

Rome Trip (Putten et al., 2013)

Ave. likelihood of purchasing trip @ €170 (1 - 10)

€170 trip, missed €100
€170 trip, missed €165

25th anniversary sale — 5.95, 8.30
Regular sale — 3.40, 8.00

Condition

In the small discount condition, where the participants missed the trip priced at €165, a participant's likelihood of purchasing the same trip at a slightly higher price, regardless of the reason for the sale whether unique or regular, was fairly similar (M = 8.30 and M = 8.00 respectively). However, the likelihood of purchase for the participants who believed the sale was unique and had missed purchasing the trip for €100, the large discount condition, were significantly more likely to book the trip when they believed the original sale was a one-off (M = 5.95) than those who believed it was a more regular affair (M = 3.40).

While the way the sale was framed had no impact on those who missed a small discount, for highly discounted products the likelihood of future purchase, or influence of the inaction inertia effect, was significantly reduced when participants believed the chance of another sale was unlikely. When participants anticipated they would have a similar opportunity to purchase the trip in the future, and thus experienced a lower level of anticipated regret, they were far less likely to purchase the trip immediately after missing the discount.

The results of the experiment seem to indicate it is not just experienced regret that leads to an inaction inertia effect. Anticipated regret also plays a big part.

Task Bonus

Missed opportunities can come in many forms. Take an investor who missed the opportunity to sell shares that subsequently fell significantly in value. It is very likely that the investor will not be as willing to sell their shares in future, resulting in potentially greater losses due to the inaction inertia effect. Similarly, those who miss large bonuses at work might suffer similar negative outcomes.

In this experiment, 171 participants were given a short article to read at home before completing a reading comprehension questionnaire (Pittman & Tykocinski, 1998). The participants were given a deadline of two weeks to complete the questionnaire.

All participants were then told they would be eligible for a bonus if they completed the work within the two-week deadline. Each participant was randomly assigned one of three bonus amounts: 0.25-course credit points (small bonus), 0.5-course credit points (medium bonus), or 1-course credit point (large bonus).

Importantly, participants told that even if they submitted the questionnaire after the two-week deadline, they would still earn 1 credit point for submission. However, failure to return the completed questionnaire at all would forfeit the 1 credit point.

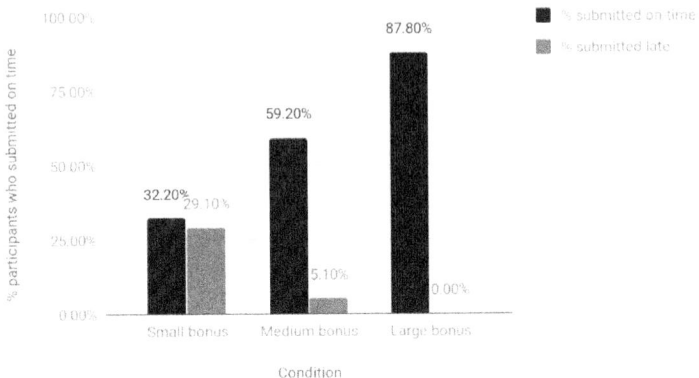

Task Bonus (Pittman & Tykocinski, 1998)

As would be expected, as the size of the bonus increased so did on-time submission rates (M = 32.2%, M = 59.2%, M = 87.8% from small to large bonus respectively). For those that submitted late, the bonus had the opposite effect. Participants realised they would no longer earn the bonus because as the size of the reward increased, the submission rate actually decreased. Again, this can be attributed to the sense of regret the participants felt believing they had "lost" the opportunity for more credits. This is completely irrational. As a result, by submitting nothing, they actually earned no points versus the 1 credit point they could have earned just for handing it in.

This finding is consistent with the previous research on the inaction inertia effect, when missing an initial attractive opportunity led to an 'irrational' inclination to avoid subsequent attractive opportunities.

Product Gems

1. **Beware of product devaluation**
   Think about your price and discounting strategy, especially during short-term price wars for generic products. You risk potential customers setting a new, inflexible expectation for great bargains.
2. **Make sure people don't miss out**
   Many potential customers feel a sense of regret having missed a sale. Regular customers might wonder why they hadn't heard any news of a sale being held. Try to encourage uptake of discounts because the risk of losing a customer is high if they don't.
3. **Be prepared for a drop in demand**
   Finance departments take note. Discounted products might boost revenues in the short term but are likely to lead to an overall drop in sales over the medium term. Retailers should expect a significant drop in sales for products immediately after a sale ends, with demand slowly increasing again with time.
4. **Avoid price comparison**
   You want to avoid product price comparison by changing your product characteristics accordingly where possible. Clothing retailers are especially good at this. The same summer t-shirt could make a great winter base layer. Customers who saw the same t-shirt in the summer sale will not devalue the product now it is framed as a winter garment and therefore will happily pay full price for it. The same idea holds true when designing a premium product when cheaper options are already available, whether your own or those of your competitors.

5. **Consider timings**

   Customers can suffer inaction inertia due to anticipated regret. If you hold regular sales, customers might wait until the product they want goes back on sale, even more so if the discount they anticipate is a large one. On the other hand, one-off or scarcely held sales for unique products will result in lower anticipated regret as customers believe the same opportunity is unlikely to come around again.

6. **Don't let customers wallow in regret**

   Regret can weigh heavy on our minds. Missed opportunities can result in lost sales, and even worse, potential customers who go elsewhere. Think about ways to minimise the damage by reducing the level of regret your potential customers' experience. Year-round price-matching strategies are a good example of one way to do this.

7. **Bonuses and incentives can be dangerous**

   As observed in the final experiment, missed targets can lead to an 'irrational' inclination to avoid subsequent attractive opportunities. Employees who miss bonuses might suffer from a significant drop in productivity immediately afterwards. Perhaps consider a graded bonus structure, where the incentives reduce gradually after a target is missed.

14. Trivialisation Effect

We prefer a thank-you over a small monetary reward

By acknowledging a customer's loyalty with a minor financial gift, we shift their perception of the relationship to a trivial, transaction-based one.

Some years ago, I helped a friend move into their first home. Their entire collection of possessions could be carried in a single suitcase, which made moving relatively simple. It did, however, make the relatively small rooms of their new house appear enormous. Apparently, that's a good thing if you're selling a house, though much less practical when you're sleeping on the floor each night.

Being a good friend, I offered to help pick out some furniture to make the house liveable. After more trips to IKEA than I can remember, spirited debate (arguments) over the assembly instructions, and litres of tea, we had finally managed to make the house liveable.

Then something weird happened. As I was leaving, my friend offered a small amount of money to repay me for giving up my weekend. I politely declined, in what was a very awkward exchange of words. On the way home, it left me wondering why they had offered me the money. It was something I'd never expected, nor experienced before.

This is a great example of what research calls the trivialisation effect; an overemphasis on rewarding customers in a minor, transactional fashion can dangerously weaken the bond between you and your loyal customer. Or, between me and my friend.

It has long been known words have an effect of trivialising, of making something smaller and less important than it really is. When we add money to a relationship, we start to think about it both in terms of the financial as well as the verbal—a double whammy of expectations, if you will.

Microsoft Points

Currently, it's popular for companies to provide small financial benefits to loyal customers, done on the expectation that it'll make them feel more appreciated. So, it follows that when gratitude is shared appropriately, consumers will be keen to have a deeper relationship with a company.

The Microsoft Xbox marketing team tried to leverage this idea in 2013, although it didn't go to plan. In fact, far from it. A promotion was launched that gave Xbox users 20 Microsoft points, a digital currency issued by Microsoft that could be used to purchase a range of digital goods. There were a number of criticisms of this since discontinued digital currency, not least because points were deceptive in terms of actual real-world cost. 79 Microsoft Points was, at one point, worth about $0.99 USD.

Some back-of-the-napkin math shows Microsoft's birthday present of 20 Microsoft points was worth just $0.25! "Don't spend it all at once", "100 more years and I can buy a game" and "thanks Microsoft!" are just a few of the sarcastic comments posted in the very public Xbox forums.

Microsoft got it wrong. In this instance no reward, the status quo, or simply saying "thank you" would have been better than all the negative press garnered from offering such a relatively small sum to reward users.

We reject "petty" financial rewards that do not meet our expectations. When we do accept them, it can have a negative impact on our satisfaction.

Hotel Stay

One of the first paper's exploring how financial acknowledgement can lead to less positive outcomes than offering a verbal acknowledgement, coined the term, trivialisation effect.

In this experiment, forty-nine participants, all guests of a hotel conference centre, were asked to provide feedback about a recent stay (Liu et al., 2015). Each participant was asked to write a review of their stay. The participants were divided into two groups. One group received a written acknowledgement thanking them for their time and feedback, while the second group received the same note, but they were also promised $0.05 to thank them for their assistance.

Once they had completed the questionnaire, participants were then asked to indicate the degree to which they felt appreciated on a 7-point scale from 1 (not at all appreciated) to 7 (very much appreciated).

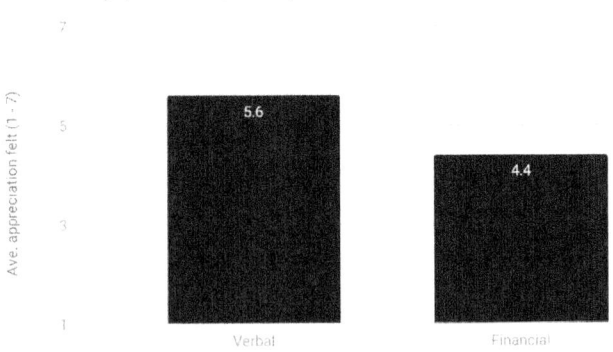

Hotel Stay (Liu et al., 2015)

Out of a maximum score of 7, those given a verbal thank-you felt a higher level of appreciation (M = 5.6) than those given the monetary reward (M = 4.4). The researchers repeated the same experiment in a restaurant setting and found the same pattern of results.

People felt more appreciated when being thanked verbally for their feedback over being given a small monetary reward.

Clothing Store (part 1)

Of course, the closer a company is to meeting these expectations around financial rewards, the more satisfied customers will be. There are not many situations where a very large financial reward would disappoint (initially). Though it begs the question: how do we evaluate a reward?

In another experiment, 364 people were asked to imagine being customers of a clothing store (Liu et al., 2015). They were all asked to assume that they spend a decent amount of money there, as well as bringing in others to the store. In essence, they were a loyal customer.

They were then shown a thank-you email sent to them by the clothing company. In each email, the participants were thanked, some verbally, some financially. The participants were split into nine groups with the size of the discount for their next purchase varying from 0% (a simple thank-you) to 40% off, in 5% increments.

After seeing this email, they were asked to rate how appreciated they felt on a 7-point scale from 1 (not at all appreciated) to 7 (very much appreciated).

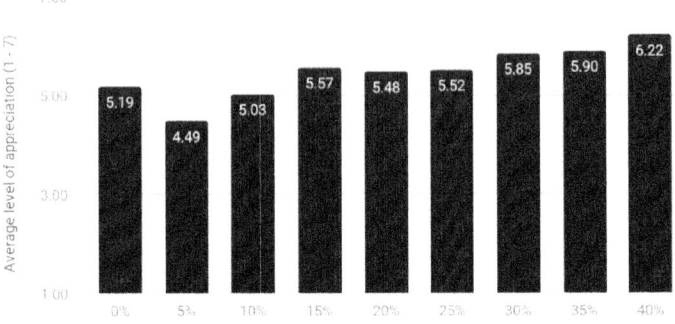

Clothing Store (part 1) (Liu et al., 2015)

One-off discount reward

Customers receiving no monetary discount felt more appreciated (M = 5.19) than those receiving the 5% (M = 4.49) or 10% (M = 5.03) discounts. The level of appreciation steadily rose alongside the level of discount given. When a 40% discount was offered the level of appreciation, as expected, was at its maximum (M = 6.22).

The results show that customers will feel more appreciated when no reward is offered in place of a small one. Increasing the reward given in-line with customer expectation will eventually remove the trivialisation effect.

Clothing Store (part 2)

Part 1 of the clothing store experiment suggests that consumers may automatically use their own financial benchmarks, or minimum satisfactory reward when financial benefits are presented. Though the question remains: how do consumers determine the value of what they deem satisfactory?

This time 251 different participants were told to imagine the same clothing store scenario covered in part 1 (Liu et al., 2015). In this experiment, the participants were split into three groups. One group was simply given a verbal thank-you. The second group of participants were told they received a 5% discount. The participants in the third—and final—group were also told they had also received a 5% discount; however, in this instance, it was framed alongside lower possible discounts; 1%, 2%, 3%, 4%, with the 5% discount circled.

As in the two preceding experiments, participants were then asked to rate how appreciated they felt on a 7-point scale from 1 from (not at all appreciated) to 7 (very much appreciated).

Clothing Store (part 2) (Liu et al., 2015)

As expected, the results replicated the trivialisation effects already observed. When participants were asked how appreciated they felt out of 7, the verbal thank-you left them feeling significantly more appreciated (M = 5.08) than the 5% discount (M = 4.25).

Interestingly, in the group where the 5% discount was framed alongside lower possible outcomes, the average appreciation reported was similar to that reported from those given the verbal thank-you (M = 5.04). Researchers believed the lower discount values shown in the note made the participants think they were in the top group of customers who received the highest possible discount (see: lucky loyalty effect).

Consumer sense of appreciation was improved without increasing the amount of money invested in a rewards program. Merely reframing existing rewards is enough to make a difference in consumer satisfaction.

Website Reviews

Financial incentives generally end up in the consumer's pocket. Cash-back schemes are a good example of this. Although researchers wondered whether morality had an impact on the effect too.

In a fourth experiment, 238 participants were asked to review a website for a tableware (furniture) company (Liu et al., 2015). Participants were first told to spend some time viewing the website and then write a review when ready.

After submitting their review, each participant was thanked for their feedback. Participants were split into four groups and depending on the group the type of thank-you they received varied:

1. A note that thanked them verbally;
2. A note that thanked them and gave them a $0.01 bonus;

3. A note that thanked them and gave them a $0.01 bonus that the company acknowledged could not begin to compensate them for their time; or
4. A note that thanked them and a $0.01 reward that was donated to charity.

Finally, participants were asked to rate how appreciated they felt on a 7-point scale from 1 from (not at all appreciated) to 7 (very much appreciated).

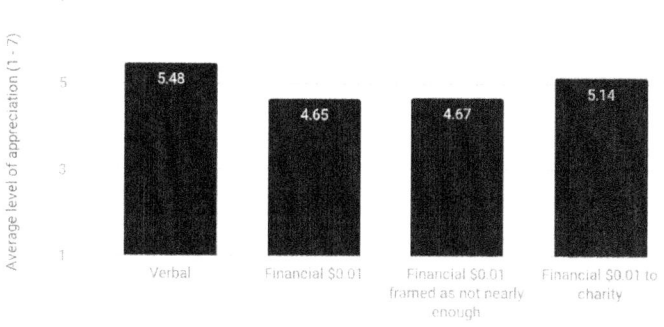

Website Reviews (Liu et al., 2015)

The participants who received the verbal acknowledgement reported the highest level of appreciation of all four groups (M = 5.48). The participants in the $0.01 reward group reported levels of appreciation almost 20% lower than the verbal group (M = 4.65). In this case, it did not matter when the $0.01 reward was framed differently (as a task that could not begin to be compensated) with similar levels of appreciation reported as the other $0.01 reward group (M = 4.67).

It would appear the trivialisation effect is minimised when the financial reward was prosocial. When the reward was given to charity on their behalf, participants reported higher levels of appreciation than the two other financial reward groups (M = 5.14).

By allowing consumers to pass on a minor financial reward to charity, appreciation, goodwill and a sense of giving are fostered.

Product Gems

1. **Keep it simple**
    Know that communicating a simple, genuine verbal appreciation to customers that conforms to verbal norms is incredibly important for your brand. While your mother might have already drilled you to say thank you, you'd be surprised the number of companies that I've seen end interactions without these simple, but expected two words.

2. **A verbal thank-you is often best**
    Thanking customers for an order, taking time out of their day to speak to you or just downloading a product brochure are all great example of where you can introduce a sense of appreciation. Don't complicate it by introducing financial rewards where possible, let Microsoft be a lesson for you.

3. **Be aware of trivialising words**
    Some words have an effect of trivialising, of making something smaller and less important than it really is. Trivialisation is often used in negotiations to make what you want seem smaller. For example, "it's not very expensive for what you are getting".

4. **Timing is everything**
    You should think about when and how often you show your appreciation to consumers. Research suggests the timing of the thank-you may be more important than the frequency of these acknowledgements (Hsee et al., 2015). Ensure acknowledgements or rewards quickly follow desired customer behaviour. Similarly, also communicate to customers the connection between their desired behaviour and the acknowledgement.

5. **Know your prospect**
    If you plan to introduce financial rewards, perhaps a

discount coupon for shoppers, first understand what their expected levels of financial reward are. Indeed, money can be beneficial in acknowledging loyalty, but being aware of how much is crucial. As the experiments show, you need to offer something above a customer's minimum satisfactory reward. Anything less and you'll likely see a poor uptake of the promotion, or even worse, a lower sense of customer appreciation.

6. **Frame rewards carefully**

   As the second part of the clothing store experiment shows us, simply showing the reward on a scale can change how a customer perceives it. Instead of giving out 5% discounts, let a customer know they have qualified for the highest reward tier of 5%. This will anchor the reward (see: anchoring bias) while increasing the appreciation felt and perceived reward value (see: lucky loyalty effect).

7. **Consider prosocial rewards**

   Although this won't work for all businesses, think about ways you could donate rewards to charity. In many cases, this might communicate a company's acknowledgement of success. A growing example of this is people on social media offering to donate money to charity if they can obtain a certain number of followers, "retweets" or "likes" (see: prosocial effect).

Thank you for reading this chapter!

15. Prosocial Effect

We believe caring companies create superior products

Corporate social goodwill can dramatically improve consumers' perceptions of a company's products and lead to increased sales, but only when such acts are seen as genuine.

The landscape of business is changing. In 2007, the concept of Benefit Corporations was introduced. Certified B Corporations are social enterprises verified by B Lab, a non-profit organisation, based on how they create value for non-shareholding stakeholders, such as their employees, the local community, and the environment.

Since the first generation of B Corporations were certified, the number of firms earning certification has grown exponentially ever since. In 2016, there were at least 1,863 certified B Corporations across 130 industries in fifty countries. Some of the most well-known B Corporations include Patagonia, Ben & Jerry's and Etsy.

Many would agree that companies that actively engage in acts of social responsibility have a better reputation in the eyes of customers and the wider community than those who don't. Perhaps surprisingly, social goodwill can also increase the perceived quality of a product too.

Done correctly, socially responsible companies, from technology to food, can deliver significantly better product evaluations and sales performance with consumers rewarding their good intentions.

Patagonia

In the 1950s, pioneering rock climber Yvon Chouinard started making equipment to replace pitons, the metal spikes that caused damage to rock faces. For climbers, it was like religion—they were messing up their own church.

The new style of equipment invented by Chouinard not only protected the rock but also led to increased sales for his company, Patagonia.

In the mid-1990s, there was a shortage of organic cotton—cotton that Patagonia relied on to make its products. While other companies might source non-organic alternatives in the interim, Chouinard's' response was "if we have to be in business using an evil product like traditionally grown cotton, we don't deserve to be in business".

The big 'a-ha' for Chouinard was that you could do something good for the environment that was also good for your business. Patagonia became California's first B Corporation in January 2012. At the time, the company was turning over $600m in annual revenues and employed around 2000 people.

Patagonia continues to donate 10% of its profits to small-scale environmental campaigns where $10,000-$15,000 can make a real difference. Their Worn Wear initiative encourages the repair, recycling and resale of garments. The company once took a full-page advert in the New York Times with the tagline: "don't buy this jacket, unless you really need it".

From 2008 to 2014, the company tripled its profits. The brand is widely known and hunted out by customers

the world over. The cause? Their customers believe the company's products are superior to others in the market, in large part down to their acts of social responsibility.

Wine Tasting

A survey of senior managers found 86% believed that acts of company kindness wouldn't affect perceived product performance. Researchers wanted to examine if this was actually the case; whether a company's level of social responsibility can have a positive impact on consumer perceptions of their products performance.

Fifty-six participants were asked to taste a single type of red wine in an unmarked plastic cup (Chernev & Blair, 2015). The participants were split into two groups.

One group were shown a card explaining more about the winery that produced the wine they were tasting (no social responsibility). The second group was shown the same card; however, the card they were given also informed them that the winery engaged in socially responsible activities (socially responsible). Specifically, these participants were told that the winery donates 10% of its sales revenues to the American Heart Association.

After reading and tasting the wine, both groups were asked to rate the wines taste on a 9-point scale from 1 (very bad) to 9 (very good). Participants were also asked to rate how much they knew about wine on a similar 9-point scale from 1 (very little) to 9 (very much).

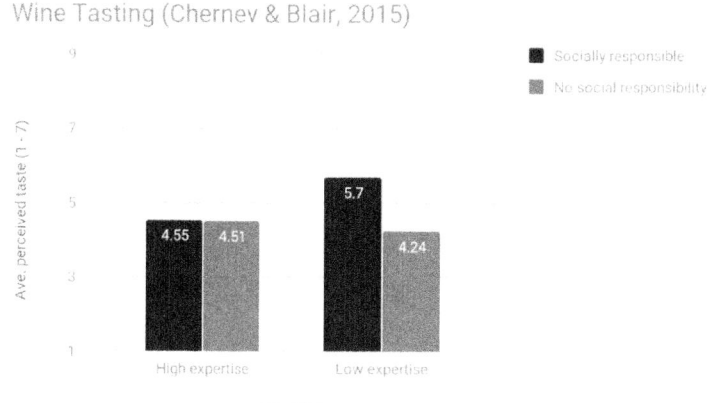
Wine Tasting (Chernev & Blair, 2015)

When looking at the results, researchers found participants with a self-confessed high-expertise of wine, wine connoisseurs if you will, rated the taste only slightly better when they knew the company was donating 10% of its sales revenues to charity (M = 4.55) than when they were not given this information (M = 4.51).

Astonishingly, those participants who reported a low-expertise in wines rated the taste significantly higher when the winery made a charitable donation (M = 5.70) to those who weren't given this information (M = 4.24).

The results suggest that acts of corporate social responsibility can strengthen consumer evaluations of a product.

Surprisingly, they also show that a company's social responsibility can have a more pronounced influence on how consumers evaluate a product when they are less familiar with it (high vs low expertise).

Hair Loss

Hopefully, the prosocial effect is already getting you to think of ways you and your organisation could improve social goodwill efforts. Though beware, it's not about quick wins. Researchers hypothesised that companies merely carrying out acts of social good that do not align to genuine morals might have no impact, or even worse, a negative impact, on a consumer's perception of their brand or product.

In another experiment, 236 participants were split into two groups (Chernev & Blair, 2015). The first group was asked what they thought about companies who donated to charity for moral reasons (moral). The other group was asked the opposite; what they thought about companies who donated to charity for selfish reasons (self-interest). This was done to prime participants about the intentions of a company during the next part of the experiment.

Participants were told that a pharmaceutical company was conducting clinical trials for a new hair-loss treatment. Half of both groups were then told the pharmaceutical company donated 20% of its revenues to charities that provide medicine to the underprivileged. The other half were not given this information.

Finally, all participants were then shown two pictures of a man's scalp that were said to be before-and-after pictures showing the results of using the company's hair loss treatment.

Participants were then asked to rate how much hair grew after the treatment on a 7-point scale from 1 (very little) to 7 (a lot).

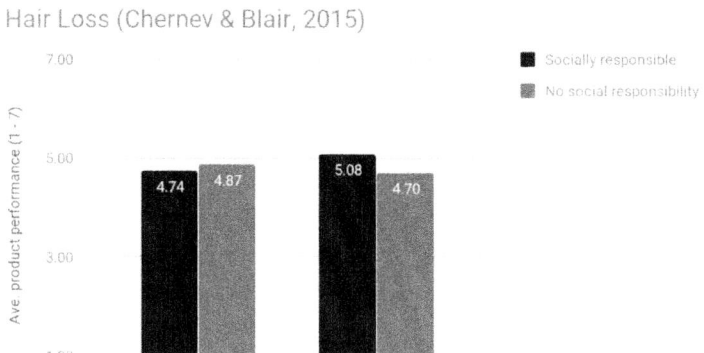

Hair Loss (Chernev & Blair, 2015)

Participants reported better regrowth for the product made by a company seen as genuinely engaging in social good (M = 5.08) versus those who donated for self-interest (M = 4.74). In fact, the participants in the group who rated product performance when the company was donating for purely selfish reasons ranked it as worse (M = 4.74) than the participants who received no information about whether the company made charitable donations (M = 4.87).

This study highlights how corporate social responsibility can bolster perceptions of product performance. Not only that, the prosocial effect is more pronounced when consumers believe that a company's motivation for engaging in prosocial behaviour is genuine rather than in pursuit of self-interest.

Simply being socially responsible for self-interest actually negatively impacted the way products were viewed, whereas genuine morals and intentions improved the way products were perceived.

Teeth Whitening

Those in sales or marketing positions reading this might agree that word of mouth is often the best form of promotion. In many cases, customers would rather choose products based on independent peer reviews than a salesperson who will be inherently biased in their opinion. With this in mind, researchers hypothesised that the same might be true of corporate social goodwill.

To test this theory, 194 participants in an experiment were told about a company, Ultradent, who are a major producer of dental products, including teeth-whitening kits (Chernev & Blair, 2015).

The participants were split into two groups with each shown two different pieces of content. The first group was shown a recent news story by an independent news organisation that monitored corporate behaviour (unbiased). In contrast, the other half were shown an excerpt taken from a recent company advertisement from Ultradent (biased).

Half of both groups were also shown a slightly longer excerpt from each of the sources that described that Ultradent made sizeable donations to UNICEF, a humanitarian organisation that provides assistance to children and mothers in developing countries.

All participants were subsequently shown two pictures of tooth images from a standard dental shade guide used by dental practitioners. These images, one shade apart on the shade guide, were described as before-and-after pictures showing the results of using Ultradent's teeth-whitening product.

After seeing the photos, participants were asked to report how well they thought the teeth-whitening product had worked on a scale from 1 (very poorly) to 7 (very well).

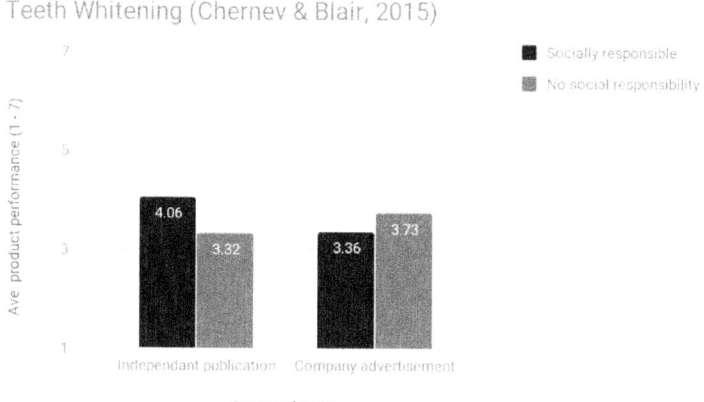

Teeth Whitening (Chernev & Blair, 2015)

Even though the pictures of teeth shown to participants were just one dental shade apart, those who learned of Ultradent's donations from an independent source believed the teeth-whitening product performed significantly better (M = 4.06) compared to those who learned of the donations via the company's own advertisement (M = 3.36). Interestingly, Ultradent's advertisement yielded better customer reviews for the product when no information about a donation to charity was included (M = 3.73).

The effect of corporate social responsibility on perceived product performance is significantly influenced by the source of the information where customers learn of socially responsible acts. When heard from a third party, customers are more likely to believe a company's motivation for engaging in socially responsible activities are genuine.

Digitised Books

Many of us give to charities that align with our self-beliefs. We make a conscious decision about who we donate time, money or effort to. A final study by the researchers looked at how the perception of products was influenced by the prosocial effect when the companies' morals aligned (or didn't) with their acts of goodwill.

In the experiment, seventy-seven participants were presented with a description of SmartScan, a fictional company that produced software that helps digitise and preserve print content by improving the resolution of text scanned from books (Chernev & Blair, 2015). This time, all participants were informed that SmartScan donates 3% of its profits to the American Cancer Society.

Participants were then split into two groups. The first was told "the company continued its charitable work even in the toughest economic times because giving back to society was aligned with their values" (moral). In contrast, the second group of participants were told that donating was really just about Smartscan's public image, and it only cared about generating positive publicity (self-interest).

Each participant, regardless of group, was then shown two sets of printed letters; one of low-resolution, the other of high-resolution. The lower resolution text was labelled "Without SmartScan," and the higher resolution text was labelled "With SmartScan".

They were then asked how much SmartScan improved the text resolution on a 7-point scale from 1 (Not at all) to 7 (Very much). Participants were also asked a second question: "How important do you think it is for companies to give back to society?" Again, they were told to report their answer on a 7-point scale from 1 (Not at all important) to 7 (Very important).

Digitised Books (Chernev & Blair, 2015)

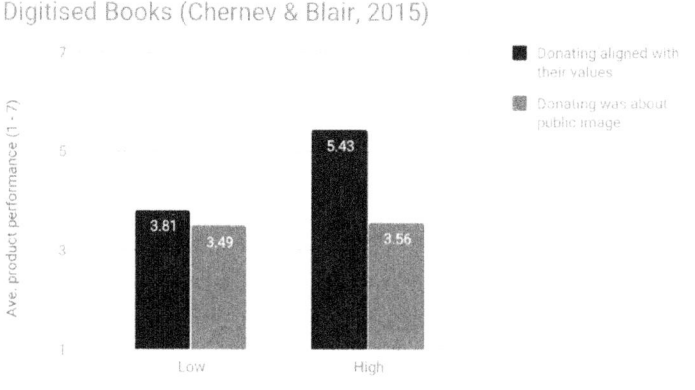

As expected, when participants believed it was important for companies to give back to society, product performance was rated as better (M = 5.43) than those who didn't (M = 3.81) when the donation made aligned to the SmartScan's core values.

It is also worth pointing out that regardless of the person's moral expectations, the company that gave back to society for moral reasons was consistently rated better (M = 3.81 and M = 5.43) than when just giving for reasons of self-interest (M = 3.49 and M = 3.56).

Participants rated the quality of the company's product higher when acts of goodwill aligned with the company's moral values instead of the company's self-image.

Product Gems

1. **Do (good) business**
   If you do decide to consider prosocial initiatives, know that in addition to benefiting society, your products will be seen as more superior, despite what most companies currently think. And better products often lead to better sales.

2. **Be genuine**
   If you take one thing away from this chapter; only genuine acts of goodwill, those that align with your own and organisations morals will reap the benefits of the prosocial effect.

3. **More effective for certain products**
   The prosocial effect worked better for those who had little knowledge about wine tasting when compared to self-confessed wine "experts". If you're launching a new product into a new market, or just have a particularly complex offering (e.g. insurance), the prosocial effect could be invaluable in shaping customer perception.

4. **It's not only about monetary donations**
   Social governance, workers, community, the environment, as well as the product or service the company provides are what aspiring B Corps are judged on. Instead of donating to charity, perhaps think about improving staff perks or organising local projects to improve the spaces around your offices. These are almost always seen as more genuine than simply handing over money.

5. **Shared morals are important**
   Think; is there a particularly common cause that aligns with your customers? Pet food customers will likely have a love for animals. As such, acts of goodwill by pet food manufacturers towards animal

protection charities will be highly regarded by their customer base, and thus the prosocial effect will be more pronounced.

6. **Works for all product types**

   In the studies above, the prosocial effect has been found to hold significant sway across a variety of product types. The same outcome is observed for virtual products too. In recent years, highly successful technology companies like Google, Facebook, VMWare, Workday, Splunk, Zynga, Salesforce, Box and Atlassian, among many others, have seen many benefits to their core business from social goodwill initiatives.

7. **Foster communication about your brand**

   As shown in the teeth-whitening experiment, word of mouth is a powerful form to promote your socially responsible efforts. Although it is easier said than done, working with an existing charity who can endorse your socially responsible credentials will be an incredibly powerful driver of the prosocial effect. Beware, paid advertising for the same activity can actually cause brand damage.

8. **Become a B Corporation**

   Becoming a B Corporation won't suit every business, not least because of the effort required to meet strict certification criteria. However, those looking to stake their claim as a force for good will find repositioning your organisation as one that aims to solve more meaningful problems can be well worth the effort in terms of benefits to society, your brand, and the consumer perception of your products.

16. Conclusion

In the same way that diamonds are abundant on earth, so too are the number of biases we as humans fall victim to. Wikipedia lists over one hundred cognitive biases from the ambiguity effect, our tendency to avoid options for which missing information makes the probability seem "unknown", to the zero-sum bias, a bias whereby a situation is incorrectly perceived to be like a zero-sum game (i.e., one-person gains at the expense of another).

Having spent many hours reading academic literature and exploring the way we make decisions, my irrational brain still keeps me from getting it right much of the time. Our inherent biases will always affect our decisions, behaviours, and memories.

While you might put down this book thinking of ways to turn things into a science experiment, remember, it's a process. Implementing all the *gems* in this book won't, on its own, lead to the next Patagonia, Amazon, or Netflix. But it will help you take a step in the right direction to build products people love.

Acknowledgements

This book would not have been possible without the support of my parents, Christopher and Alison, who allowed me to use their quiet study, now writing room, for many long nights spent researching and writing. Thank you for allowing me as a child to stay blissfully unaware of the world of adults for as long as you did, and then telling me the truth about it when I finally asked. A special mention to my Dad who inspired many of the examples cited in this book. You're not really the most irrational person I know, *most of the time.*

References

1. Foot-in-the-Door Technique

L. Freedman, Jonathan & C. Fraser, Scott. (1966). Compliance Without Pressure: The Foot-in-the-Door Technique. Journal of personality and social psychology. 4. 195-202. 10.1037/h0023552.

Scott, Carol. (1977). Modifying Socially-Conscious Behavior: The Foot-in-the-Door Technique. Journal of Consumer Research - J CONSUM RES. 4. . 10.1086/208691.

Grassini, Aude & Pascual, Alexandre & Guéguen, Nicolas. (2013). The Effect of the Foot-in-the-Door Technique on Sales in a Computer-Mediated Field Setting. Communication Research Reports. 30. 63-67. 10.1080/08824096.2012.746223.

2. Category Size Bias

Isaac, Mathew & Brough, Aaron. (2014). Judging a Part by the Size of Its Whole: The Category Size Bias in Probability Judgments. Journal of Consumer Research. 41. 2014. 10.1086/676126.

3. Choice Paradox

Schwartz (2009). The Paradox of Choice: Why More Is Less. HarperCollins.

S. Iyengar, Sheena & Lepper, Mark. (2001). When Choice is Demotivating: Can One Desire Too Much of a Good

Thing?. Journal of personality and social psychology. 79. 995-1006. 10.1037/0022-3514.79.6.995.

Zeelenberg, Marcel & Beattie, Jane. (1997). Consequences of Regret Aversion 2: Additional Evidence for Effects of Feedback on Decision Making. Organizational Behavior and Human Decision Processes. 72. 63-78. 10.1006/obhd.1997.2730.

Shiner, Rebecca. (2015). Maximizers, Satisficers, and Their Satisfaction With and Preferences for Reversible Versus Irreversible Decisions. Social Psychological and Personality Science. 6. . 10.1177/1948550615595271.

4. Choice-Supportive Bias

Bahrick, Harry & Hall, Lynda & Berger, Stephanie. (1996). Accuracy and Distortion in Memory for High School Grades. Psychological Science - PSYCHOL SCI. 7. 265-271. 10.1111/j.1467-9280.1996.tb00372.x.

Bahrick, Harry & Hall, Lynda & A Da Costa, Laura. (2008). Fifty Years of Memory of College Grades: Accuracy and Distortions. Emotion (Washington, D.C.). 8. 13-22. 10.1037/1528-3542.8.1.13.

Mather, Mara & Shafir, E & K Johnson, M. (2000). Misremembrance of Options Past: Source Monitoring and Choice. Psychological science. 11. 132-8. 10.1111/1467-9280.00228.

Cialdini, Robert. (2009). The Psychology of Persuasion.

Mather, Mara & K. Johnson, Marcia. (2001). Choice-supportive source monitoring: Do our decisions seem better to us as we age?. Psychology and aging. 15. 596-606. 10.1037/0882-7974.15.4.596.

Henkel, Linda & Mather, Mara. (2007). Memory attributions for choices: How beliefs shape our memories. Journal of Memory and Language. 57. 163-176. 10.1016/j.jml.2006.08.012.

5. Centre-Stage Effect

Valenzuela, Ana & Raghubir, Priya. (2009). Position-based beliefs: The center-stage effect. Journal of Consumer Psychology - J CONSUM PSYCHOL. 19. 185-196. 10.1016/j.jcps.2009.02.011.

Nicholls, Michael (Mike & Orr, Catherine & Okubo, Matia & Loftus, Andrea. (2007). Satisfaction guaranteed: The effect of spatial biases on responses to Likert scales. Psychological science. 17. 1027-8. 10.1111/j.1467-9280.2006.01822.x.

Rodway, Paul & Schepman, Astrid & Lambert, Jordana. (2012). Preferring the One in the Middle: Further Evidence for the Centre-stage Effect. Applied Cognitive Psychology. 26. 215 - 222. 10.1002/acp.1812.

6. Status Quo Bias

Samuelson, W.; Zeckhauser, R. (1988). Status quo bias in decision-making. Journal of Risk and Uncertainty. 1: 7–59.10.1007/bf00055564.

7. Social Default Bias

J. Goldstein, Noah & Cialdini, Robert & Griskevicius, Vladas. (2008). A Room With a Viewpoint: Using Social Norms to Motivate Environmental Conservation in Hotels. Journal of Consumer Research. 35. 472-482. 10.1086/586910.

Burnkrant, Robert & Cousineau, Alain. (1975). Informational and Normative Social Influence in Buyer Behavior. Journal of Consumer Research. 2. 206-15. 10.1086/208633.

Eun Huh, Young & Vosgerau, Joachim & Morewedge, Carey. (2014). Social Defaults: Observed Choices Become Choice Defaults. Journal of Consumer Research. 41. 10.1086/677315.

Deutsch, Morton & B Gerard, Harold. (1955). A Study of Normative and Informational Influences upon Individual Judgment. Journal of Abnormal and Social Psychology. 51. 629-36.

S. Baron, Robert & A. Vandello, Joseph & Brunsman, Bethany. (1996). The Forgotten Variable in Conformity Research: Impact of Task Importance on Social Influence. Journal of Personality and Social Psychology. 71. 915-927. 10.1037/0022-3514.71.5.915.

Cialdini, Robert & J. Demaine, Linda & Sagarin, Brad & Barrett, Daniel & Rhoads, Kelton & Winter, Patricia. (2006). Activating and Aligning Social Norms for Persuasive Impact. Psychology Press Ltd SOCIAL INFLUENCE. 1. 3-15. 10.1080/15534510500181459.

8. Availability Heuristic

Tversky, Amos & Kahneman, Daniel. (1973). Availability: A Heuristic for Judging Frequency and Probability. Cognitive Psychology. 5. 207-232. 10.1016/0010-0285(73)90033-9.

Schwarz, Norbert & Bless, Herbert & Strack, Fritz & Klumpp, Gisela & Rittenauerschatka, H & Simons, Annette. (1991). Ease of Retrieval as Information - Another Look at the Availability Heuristic. Journal of Personality and Social Psychology, v.61, 195-202 (1991). 61.. 10.1037//0022-3514.61.2.195.

Vaughn, Leigh. (1999). Effects of uncertainty on use of the availability of heuristic for self-efficacy judgments. European Journal of Social Psychology. 29.. 10.1002/(SICI)1099-0992(199903/05)29:2/33.0.CO;2-3.

9. Anchoring Bias

Tversky, A & Kahneman, Daniel. (1974). Judgment under uncertainty: heuristics and biases. Biases in judgments reveal some heuristics of thinking under uncertainty. Science. 185. 1124-1131.

Ariely, Dan & Loewenstein, George & Prelec, Drazen. (2005). Tom Sawyer and the Construction of Value. SSRN Electronic Journal. . 10.2139/ssrn.774970.

Strack, Fritz & Mussweiler, Thomas. (1997). Explaining the Enigmatic Anchoring Effect: Mechanisms of Selective Accessibility. Journal of Personality and Social Psychology. 73. 437-446. 10.1037/0022-3514.73.3.437.

Cialdini, Robert & E. Vincent, Joyce & K. Lewis, Stephen & Catalan, Jose & Wheeler, Diane & Lee Darby, Betty. (1975). Reciprocal concessions procedure for inducing compliance: The Door-in-the-Face technique. Journal of Personality and Social Psychology. 31. 206-215. 10.1037/h0076284.

Bergman, Oscar & Ellingsen, Tore & Johannesson, Magnus & Svensson, Cicek. (2010). Anchoring and Cognitive Ability. Economics Letters. 107. 66-68. 10.1016/j.econlet.2009.12.028.

Alevy, Jonathan & Landry, Craig & List, John. (2010). Field Experiments on Anchoring of Economic Valuations. Economic Inquiry. 53. . 10.2139/ssrn.1824400.

10. Picture Superiority Effect

Clark, Jim & Paivio, Allan. (1987). A Dual Coding Perspective on Encoding Processes. 5-33. 10.1007/978-1-4612-4676-3_1.

Childers, Terry & Houston, Michael. (1984). Conditions for a Picture-Superiority Effect on Consumer Memory. Journal of Consumer Research - J CONSUM RES. 11. 10.1086/209001.

Intraub, Helene & Nicklos, Susan. (1985). Levels of Processing and Picture Memory. The Physical Superiority Effect. Journal of experimental psychology. Learning, memory, and cognition. 11. 284-98. 10.1037//0278-7393.11.2.284.

Atkinson, Richard & Shiffrin, Richard. (1968). "Chapter: Human memory: A proposed system and its control processes".

Grant E. Donnelly, Laura Y. Zatz, Dan Svirsky, Leslie K. John. (2018). "The Effect of Graphic Warnings on Sugary Drink Purchasing,", Psychological Science. 10.1177/0956797618766361

Bolen, William. (1984). Advertising.

Schultz, Don E. (1981), Essentials of Advertising Strategy. Chicago: Crain Books.

11. Scarcity Bias

Worchel, Stephen & Lee, Jerry & Adewole, Akanbi. (1975). Effects of supply and demand on object value. Journal of Personality and Social Psychology. 32. 906-914. 10.1037/0022-3514.32.5.906.

Wansink, Brian & J Kent, Robert & J Hoch, Stephen. (1998). An Anchoring and Adjustment Model of Purchase Quantity Decisions. Journal of Marketing Research. 35. 71-81. 10.2307/3151931?ref=no-x-route:e1f563acdfe5bc4cf0d4d4b225bb7157.

Deng, Changrong & Pekec, Sasa (2013). Optimal Allocation of Exclusivity Contracts.

12. Peak-End Rule

Kahneman, Daniel & L. Fredrickson, Barbara & A. Schreiber, Charles & A. Redelmeier, Donald. (1993). When

More Pain is Preferred to Less—Adding a Better End. Psychological Science. 4. . 10.1111/j.1467-9280.1993.tb00589.x.

A Redelmeier, Donald & Kahneman, Daniel. (1996). Patients' memories of painful medical treatments: Real-time and retrospective evaluations of two minimally invasive procedures. Pain. 66. 3-8. 10.1016/0304-3959(96)02994-6.

Do, Amy & V Rupert, Alexander & Wolford, George. (2008). Evaluations of Pleasurable Experiences: The Peak-End Rule. Psychonomic bulletin & review. 15. 96-8. 10.3758/PBR.15.1.96

13. Inaction Inertia Effect

Arkes, Hal & Kung, Yi-Han & Hutzel, Laura. (2002). Regret, Valuation, and Inaction Inertia. Organizational Behavior and Human Decision Processes. 87. 371-385. 10.1006/obhd.2001.2978.

Putten, Marijke & Zeelenberg, Marcel & van Dijk, Eric. (2013). How consumers deal with missed discounts: Transaction decoupling, action orientation and inaction inertia. Journal of Economic Psychology. 38. 104–110. 10.1016/j.joep.2012.09.008.

Tykocinski, Orit & Pittman, Thane. (1998). The Consequences of Doing Nothing: Inaction Inertia as Avoidance of Anticipated Counterfactual Regret. Journal of Personality and Social Psychology. 75. 607-616. 10.1037/0022-3514.75.3.607.

14. Trivialisation Effect

Liu, Peggy & Lamberton, Cait & L. Haws, Kelly. (2015). Should Firms Use Small Financial Benefits to Express Appreciation to Consumers? Understanding and Avoiding Trivialization Effects. Journal of Marketing. 79. 74-90. 10.1509/jm.14.0091.

K. Hsee, Christopher & Yang, Yang & Ruan, Bowen. (2015). The Mere Reaction Effect: Even Non-positive and Non-informative Reactions Can Reinforce Actions. Journal of Consumer Research. . . 10.1093/jcr/ucv022.

15. Prosocial Effect

Chernev, Alexander & Blair, Sean. (2015). Doing Well by Doing Good: The Benevolent Halo of Corporate Social Responsibility. Journal of Consumer Research. 41. 000-000. 10.1086/680089.

One Final Gem

Have you seen the Product Gems Behavioural Science Card Deck?

The card deck is a collection of 40 flashcards that each distil a piece of behavioural science research into easy-to-understand *gems* suggesting ways to apply the findings to the design of your products.

Visit

PRODUCTGEMS.IO

to find out more about the card deck, all the other books in the Product Gems series, and much, much more.

Printed in Great Britain
by Amazon

68294847R00132